All of us will hit the wall; it's just a matter of time. And, when we do, there's no "quick fix." Ryan Rush is a passionate storyteller, and woven between his very personal stories is a challenge for each of us to experience a Faith Breakthrough. He offers no neat formulas but life-changing principles.

**VERNON BREWER**
President/CEO, World Help

My friend Ryan Rush is one of the most effective voices I know in helping individuals and families move beyond obstacles to experience spiritual breakthroughs. Read *Walls* to discover why.

**KURT BRUNER**
Pastor of spiritual formation, Lake Pointe Church; author of *It Starts at Home*

Ryan knows what it takes to break through walls, both from his personal experience and as a pastor who has helped many bust down those invisible barriers that hold them back from God's best. This book can help you identify and push past the most imposing wall in your own life.

**JOHN BURKE**
Author of *No Perfect People Allowed: Creating a Come-as-You-Are Culture in the Church*

As the walls of Jericho crumbled by the power of God, so do the walls in our lives, which keep us from experiencing all God has for us. With grace and precision, Ryan Rush shows us that escape from our man-made prisons is not found in physical fortitude but in a poverty of spirit that trusts in the only One who can set us free.

**MATT CARTER**
Lead pastor, Austin Stone Community Church

Authentic. Relevant. Humble. Passionate Christ-follower. Put those together, and you get Ryan Rush. Read *Walls* and get ready to say goodbye to yours.

**WILL DAVIS JR.**
Lead pastor, Austin Christian Fellowship; author of *Pray Big*

Ryan, a gifted storyteller, reveals our tendency to be masterful wall builders. He brings us face to face with the walls we unknowingly build. He then reveals the biblical principles available to us when we decide to put on the demolition hat and go to work tearing them down.

**RON HUNTER JR.**
Coauthor of *Toy Box L[...]* [...]ce; executive director and CEO, Ra[...]

*Walls* will help you make sense out of this beautiful mess we call "under the sun" living. Ryan's fresh and humble approach to life's obstacles is refreshing and rewarding. This book will change your life!

**RANDY PHILLIPS**
Phillips, Craig & Dean; lead pastor, Promiseland West

*Walls* is a practical and honest book that connects faith with reality. This book will change lives.

**KEN DAVIS**
Author, speaker, consultant

Using a dynamic and motivating approach, Pastor Ryan reveals both how to reach heaven and how to live on earth. *Walls* is a constructive and enlightening book that explains how to overcome obstacles using two key elements: faith and action. After reading this book, you will never again be a mere dreamer but will become a dream maker.

**CARLOS VARGAS**
Founder of Hope of Life International, Guatemala

After stepping on a land mine that ripped both legs from my body during the Vietnam War, I was sent to a naval hospital, where I saw much bitterness and anger. What happened to so many on that hospital ward is emblematic of what so many people in our churches experience. People get in a rut, and life seems hopeless. Well, the good news is there *is* hope. Without suggesting it's easy to get out of the rut, Ryan Rush explains the biblical way to escape. This book is a must-read for *everyone* in the church!

**TIM LEE**
Evangelist

When God brought a "barrier wall" into Ryan's life, he forced Ryan to go deeper in Jesus Christ than ever before. Before God could use him in ministry, Ryan had to learn his own limitations, understand the power of God, and discover that all our resources are in Jesus Christ. As God changed Ryan Rush, may He change you.

**DR. ELMER L. TOWNS**
Cofounder and vice president, Liberty University; dean, Liberty Baptist Theological Seminary and School of Religion

Ryan's vulnerability is timely, as many of us struggle when our faith is challenged. His biblical view on our need for a new, healthy perspective is freeing! If you are facing a tough situation, this book is for you.

**JIM WEIDMANN**
Coauthor of *Spiritual Milestones* and *The Focus on the Family Guide to the Spiritual Growth of Children*; founder, the Family Night Movement

I love this book. *Walls* has helped me deal with personal challenges we all face in our lives. This is a book everybody should read and study.

**ART WILLIAMS**
President, the A. L. Williams Company

Ryan Rush is a powerful preacher who now displays an equal ability as an author. I predict his new book *Walls* will be an immense aid, helping readers realize, identify, and break through their unique walls.

**DR. HAROLD WILLMINGTON**
Bible teacher; author of *The Outline Bible* and *Willmington's Bible Handbook*

Some books ignite movements. I believe this is just such a book. Not only can it help you tear down the walls you're facing, it's a message and tool you'll want to share with your family, church, and community. Ryan has helped hundreds of people tear down even the most difficult walls holding them back from experiencing God's best. Let him show you how God's promises can go to work on any walls you're facing as well.

**JOHN TRENT, PH.D.**
President, StrongFamilies.com and The Institute for the Blessing at Barclay College

Ryan Rush has taken a thoughtful look at the challenges we face that can seem insurmountable at times. Without casually dismissing these hardships, he admonishes us to find, with God's help, the confidence and strength to break down the walls in our lives and to move the mountains in our paths with the sheer power of perseverance and faith.

**JERRY FALWELL JR.**
Chancellor, Liberty University

When Ryan Rush's daughter Lily is a little older, I want to meet her. I want to look her in the eyes and say, "Your life is full of meaning and purpose for a thousand reasons. But among those reasons is this—your early years enriched and refined the mind of your daddy. You helped him learn how to tell all of us how to bring down the walls in our lives through faith grounded in God's promises. Every time a wall comes down somewhere, you were part of that. I am so glad you are on earth." Each person who reads *Walls* will understand those words, and will probably stand in line with me to speak to Lily.

**RICHARD ROSS, PH.D.**
Professor of student ministry, Southwestern Seminary (www.RichardARoss.com)

Ryan Rush has clearly identified the barrier standing between the life we presently have and the life God designed us to live according to his promises. You will cry as you recognize your personal walls, and you will be overjoyed as you discover freedom, hope, and a new way of living. *Walls* is a must-read for every person feeling stuck and in desperate need of a breakthrough.

**DR. BRIAN HAYNES**
Senior pastor, Bay Area Baptist Church; author of Shift: What it Takes to Finally Reach Families Today

We all know what walls feel like—walls of discouragement, habitual sin, or deception. Pastor Rush reminds us that the truth that God has revealed to us in the pages of Scripture "can prove to be the turning point in our lives." When we take God's Word to heart, breakthroughs are not far behind!

**DR. ROB RIENOW**
Family pastor, Wheaton Bible Church; founder of Visionary Parenting (www.VisionaryParenting.com)

Authentic. Proven. Practical. Ryan's words truly empower people who feel "stuck," using real-life stories of Christ's power to create a doorway beyond the walls that hold us back. Consider this book your biblical sledge-hammer to break through the barriers that keep you from the freedom God has intended for your life.

**DANIEL HENDERSON**
President, Strategic Renewal

Walls present different challenges in the eyes of their beholder. To some, they hold captive; to others, they protect; but to the person of faith, they are to be scaled and overcome. In this delightful book, Ryan Rush chooses to overcome and encourages all who read it to accept their reality and then scale that wall to freedom.

**H. B. LONDON JR.**
Vice president, church & clergy, Focus on the Family

# WALLS

## WHY EVERYBODY'S STUCK
### (and nobody has to be)

## RYAN RUSH

 Tyndale House Publishers, Inc., Carol Stream, Illinois

**Library of Congress Cataloging-in-Publication Data**

Rush, Ryan.
    Walls : why everybody's stuck (and nobody has to be) / Ryan Rush.
        p. cm.
    Includes bibliographical references (p.    ).
    ISBN 978-1-4143-3736-4 (sc)
    1. Faith. 2. God (Christianity)—Promises. 3. Walls—Religious aspects—Christianity.
I. Title.
    BV4637.R87 2011
    234′.23—dc22                                                    2010040223

Printed in the United States of America

17   16   15   14   13   12   11
  7    6    5    4    3    2    1

*Without my wife and children, there would be no book. Your sacrifices, conversations, and living examples have given me the confidence and inspiration to stay on this course long enough to make it a reality. I love you.*

*Lana, thank you for not only walking this breakthrough path with me in recent years (and recent days!), but for allowing me to show the world some of our deepest hurts and struggles.*

*Ryley and Reagan, thank you for being such incredible young women of faith, and for making your mom and me look so smart. God has great things in store for you!*

*The ultimate dedication of* Walls, *however, would be incomplete if it were not directed toward our Lily—the one who has been through so much in her short life and taught us so much about God's promises. You are a miracle and a blessing, and our Lord has unimaginably incredible plans for your life! You have already changed ours for the better.*

# CONTENTS

## PART 3: LIVING LIFE AS A WALL BREAKER

# ACKNOWLEDGMENTS

This book would not have been possible without the emotional investment of a lot of people.

The congregation of Bannockburn Baptist Church is full of living examples that Faith Breakthroughs work. Thank you for your willingness to walk in God's promises and to walk with me as we have enjoyed this glorious experiment together.

The staff of Bannockburn Baptist Church has worked, dreamed, planned, rehashed, prayed, and cried together in asking one simple question: How can we develop a process that will allow our people to carry God's promises home? These are your ideas as much as my own. Thank you for your passion and your partnership.

Dr. John Trent's heart for the American family has had a greater impact on our culture than most will ever realize until we are in heaven. His fingerprints, insights, efforts, and wisdom are found throughout this text. I can never adequately express my gratitude for his "above and beyond" work to make this book all that it could be. Thank you for pushing me to dream bigger.

My parents and in-laws have exemplified what great parents are supposed to look like, and the legacy they have passed on to my own family went a long way in shaping our home life—and in turn, the truths in this book. Thank you for your steadfastness and love.

The entire Tyndale House family has made me feel welcome, and I will always be grateful. I have witnessed firsthand the eternal mind-set with which you carry out your mission, and I am honored to associate my ministry with yours.

# INTRODUCTION: THE DAY MY WALL BECAME REAL

This book was supposed to be about a formula for over-coming the walls that hold us back. It has been twenty years in the making.

Then I hit my own wall, and the formulas went out the window.

I have spent my entire adult life trying to help people improve their lives by connecting their spiritual journeys to their everyday existence. It has always troubled me that our home lives seem so severed from what we know of God. Most churches are fighting this battle for spiritual authenticity: we speak of God's truth and his provision, but the evidence of that faith being lived out in everyday life seems far more absent than anyone would like. I've seen fathers who claim God as their own, but neglect to love their children; young adults who were raised in good churches who simply walked away; and even senior adults who begin to drift from a passionate walk with God to a regimented set of rules.

I set out to discover a better way. That's where I came upon the exhilarating, life-giving idea of Faith Breakthroughs, which I've seen help hundreds of people face their own walls and move past them to a better life.

In the years I hammered out the concepts you'll find in this book, my family was unusual in all of the good ways. Lana and I were nearly two decades into a happy marriage. Our two daughters were loving, low maintenance, and living as much of the good life as is possible in middle school. I was pastoring a large church, with a sold-out staff behind me and pews full of great people in front of me each Sunday. Each week I got to teach men and women the 1-2-3s of making Faith Breakthroughs. Thankfully, by God's grace, we heard incredible, encouraging stories of walls coming down in everyday people's lives.

But then God brought us Lily, a surprise baby after a decade away from such things as diapers and feeding schedules.

Lily was born with a host of medical problems, including a large hole in her heart that would, without imminent open-heart surgery, eventually threaten her life. I remember thinking of how many people—even well-known pastors I'd met—had suddenly come face-to-face with a major trial and loss. For many, I knew it had made them stronger and more effective in their faith and work. I wish I could tell you that in those early days of hospital stays and sleepless nights, I heroically thanked the Lord for all the heartaches. Instead, I did something more honest. I said, "God, if this is in any way about helping me become a better father, or husband, or minister, or author, or speaker, or person . . . then I quit."

All I wanted was for the pain to go away—most of all for my precious child. But God did not give us that option. All I wanted was to keep on helping others with their walls. What I had to face were walls of my own.

So here I am.

I believe with all my heart that in the pages before you there are powerful, biblical tools you can use to tear down the walls that have kept you, or your loved ones, from living the life God intends. Unfortunately, I can no longer in good conscience write a book that promises to take all the pain away in the process.

What I can share with you is what's worked in my life. What's given us sleep on sleepless nights and hope and courage during the toughest of days. I can testify about what has torn down the spiritual walls we've faced, and what I believe can do the same for you.

If what you're looking for is a simple, painless plan, you won't find it here. If your goal is a way to break through that glass ceiling and get the promotion you just know you deserve, it may not happen. Or if what you seek is a guaranteed, "no tears" way of tearing down an uncaring spouse's walls in three easy steps, you have come to the wrong place.

But what I can give you is something richer: a new way of navigating through, and past, the challenges of life. Even past that terrible wall you're facing today. I can share with you a way to experience breakthroughs even in the midst of confusion and doubt, hardship and bitterness (yes, even bitterness, if we're honest). I can do that because I now know more about walls than I ever wanted to know, and I understand that even once-conquered walls can keep springing up again. But, with truth, they can be torn down.

It's not just my story I'll share. In this book, you'll find amazing stories of everyday people I've met in our church who have used the power of Faith Breakthroughs in their lives. People who, if you sat down and heard them share their experiences, would leave you shaking your head over how they moved from the wrong side of the wall to the freedom, life, and hope they're experiencing today. I pray these stories will leave you filled with hope and courage that your wall can be torn down as well.

*—Ryan Rush*

# 1

# FACING OUR
# WALLS

# chapter one

# YOU DON'T HAVE TO BE STUCK ANYMORE

Do you ever have the feeling that you are missing out on something important?

It's probably because you are.

You are separated from blessings so incredible, in fact, that if you realized what you were missing, you wouldn't stop until you had them in your possession. Those blessings are as real as the book you hold in your hands, and they are waiting for you! But you will never enjoy them if you remain where you are right now. You are stuck, and you don't have to be. There are walls that hold you back and keep you from living your life to the fullest. And those walls don't crumble through sincere effort or positive thinking.

I discovered through my own trials that overcoming walls

is not always that simple. For me, that struggle came from the most unlikely place.

Lily changed everything.

Lily is now a four-year-old firecracker. Her therapists have nicknamed her "the Texas Tornado" because of her uncanny combination of energy and speed. In a matter of seconds she can playfully dismantle objects that once seemed indestructible. There is no barrier from which she cannot escape, and the word *childproof* is lost on her, but she can weasel out of trouble in an instant with the most beautiful smile you've ever seen. With big, bright blue eyes and floppy brown hair, Lily is the cutest little girl you'll ever lay eyes on. We call her Lily-bird because, well, it just stuck somehow.

If you ever meet her, though, you may sense that something is not quite right. That's true. In four short years of life she has accumulated an entire file box of medical records. Lily-bird's life has been a roller-coaster ride, and the adventure isn't over yet. But the highlights and heartaches of this one adorable little girl have shaped our family more than I ever thought possible.

Lily has brought me face-to-face with my own walls. Her struggles for life caused me to question not just the beliefs I held dear, but the reasons I held on to those beliefs. My journey with her has helped me realize just how important it is for people to face the walls that hold them back.

The lessons in this book are straight from the Bible, and I am totally convinced that they are effective and true. But I'll have to admit that I underestimated their profound impact on real life until I lived them myself.

If you are like the rest of us, there's a good chance that

something has challenged your understanding of God, and there's a strong possibility that those struggles have affected every other relationship in your life. Even so, I have great news for you, news that has the power to change everything: *there is a way past the walls that are holding you back.*

But before you overcome the walls in your life, you have to understand what's happening around you that has the potential to ruin you.

You have been robbed, and you might not even know it. Millions of people throughout history have been robbed in the very same way, but that doesn't make it any more acceptable to have something taken from you that is rightfully yours.

> *There is a way past the walls that are holding you back.*

You may be like one of the unwitting victims of Albert Gonzalez. You've probably never heard of him, but there's a chance he has heard of you. Albert was the hacker behind the largest credit card theft in U.S. history, swiping data from more than 130 million accounts and making off with nearly 200 million dollars before his arrest in 2008. With that many accounts involved and that much money stolen, there is a good chance you or someone you loved was a part of that number without knowing it.

But that's not the robbery I'm talking about. I'm referring to a much larger heist with a far greater consequence.

Chances are good that at this very moment you are being robbed of a breakthrough—a breakthrough that would lead you to a life God designed you to enjoy. This breakthrough has already been promised to you. You were created to experience it, to walk in its freedom, and to comprehend its power.

Just as walls come in all shapes and sizes, so do the breakthroughs that move you beyond them. You can have a breakthrough financially and receive a raise at work. You can experience a breakthrough in a relationship and marry the person of your dreams. But a far more significant breakthrough is waiting, one that ultimately paves the way for a whole new life of victory.

This is what I call a Faith Breakthrough, and I am praying that there is one in your very near future. A Faith Breakthrough is the act of overcoming a life barrier by learning to trust in, and intentionally pursue, God and what he has promised you.

> *A Faith Breakthrough is the act of overcoming a life barrier by learning to trust in, and intentionally pursue, God and what he has promised you.*

As a pastor, daily radio show host, and national speaker, I have had the privilege of coming into contact with tens of thousands of people across America, and I have yet to meet someone who hasn't faced walls. It turns out, as far as I can tell (and unless you are the first), that we are all stuck in some way. By "stuck" I mean that we tend to find ourselves caught in a place where no progress is made for an extended period of time—even when we know instinctively that more lies just ahead. This is true in our personal lives, in businesses, in churches, and in entire communities.

Of course, I have had a front-row seat to one of those groups. I have spent long days and nights trying to figure out the reasons for the frail faith of the modern church—a group of people who seem to be better at talking a good game in a building once a week than truly walking with God in daily life. I have witnessed what happens to families when parents fake their faith on Sundays and then forget it at home. I have looked at the pervasive inconsistency between most people's stated goals and their actual schedules. I grow even more frustrated when I witness the sincere desire of the wonderful people in these households to live life as they should. The inconsistency is rarely a defiant act of hypocrisy, but instead a sense of confusion about how to fix the problem or an inability to see that problem at all.

I have looked at all the "quick fixes" for home life and been left wanting more. I am convinced that the problem goes deeper than giving people a few simple lifestyle adjustments and hoping all will be better. Nope—most of us are beyond the Band-Aid phase. It's time to stop settling for business as usual and to pursue the spiritual life we've always dreamed of.

## EVERYBODY'S STUCK, AND NOBODY HAS TO BE

If we're enjoying all God really has for us, then our faith will overflow into every nook and cranny of our lives, transforming every relationship we have, every perspective we perceive, and every legacy we leave. That's the magnitude of a Faith Breakthrough—and the secret to overcoming every unseen wall that is holding us back.

I'm not promising it will be easy to face the regret of having been robbed for this long or to realize what could have been. I am only promising that you don't have to be robbed any longer if you take ownership of what God has in store for you.

Albert Gonzalez and his band of hackers were able to rob so many of so much because they were invisible to the victims. His electronic scams were taking place without detection because nobody knew he was there. It's much harder to steal something when the owner is holding it in his or her clutches and there is a sense of loss. It becomes a lot easier when the owner never knew what was missing in the first place.

Maybe you never knew you were stuck behind a wall or missing out on your breakthrough. You've heard about God's promises perhaps all of your life, but you never quite grasped just how personal they were to you—until right now. And that's why there is so much opportunity in store for you in the pages ahead.

As a pastor, there's nothing more disappointing than seeing someone I care for who has fallen victim to the lies of the enemy. I've known drug addicts who decided it was too late to change, who ultimately wrote their own death sentences. Fathers who determined they had already wasted too much of their relationships to reconcile with their grown children. Sinners who decided they were far too guilty to seek forgiveness.

They were robbed of the blessings awaiting them, distracted by the lies holding them back.

On the other hand, there is nothing more gratifying to a pastor than watching walls come crashing down.

The Carpenter family will never, ever be the same again. Brad's bout with prescription painkillers had started years earlier when he was dealing with a work-related injury, but the dependence on the pills extended far beyond the medical need and eventually dominated his thoughts, his motivations, and his very existence. After being stuck for years behind a

Wall of Discontent and Shame, Brad was about to give in to all of the pressures he was facing and run away from it all. Instead, he cried out to God—and cried out for help from some close friends in his congregation. They shared with him the truth about his walls and the opportunity he had for a genuine breakthrough. As the principles in this book began to permeate Brad's life and family, what happened next was nothing short of a miraculous transformation. I'll never forget a recent Sunday morning service when Brad told the entire church about his walls, the addiction that those walls brought about, and the powerful forces of change that had totally transformed his family, his future, and the way he looked at life. He looked out at that crowd, eyes welled up with tears, and proclaimed something to every person in that auditorium: You don't have to be stuck anymore.

Brad wants you to know the same thing, and I want you to know that there is an opportunity before you that might just be greater than you ever imagined.

Jesus warned his disciples in John 10:10 that just such a robbery was a genuine threat to them: "The thief's purpose is to steal and kill and destroy."

*You don't have to be stuck anymore.*

It is important to remember that the life you're missing out on is not being taken from you by accident. Believe it or not, the Bible tells us we have a very real enemy who is out to deceive the people God loves so dearly. You've heard him called the adversary, the devil, Satan, and Lucifer, to name a few. Just know that this enemy is real, and he has a heartless plan to rob you and leave you lifeless, trapped forever behind your own walls with all your breakthrough opportunities left in a garbage heap along the way. He is in the business of creating barriers of deception that are intended to hold you back, and many of these walls are cleverly disguised as very enticing alternatives: Comfort. Revenge. Ignorance. Entertainment. He intends to do only one thing: to con you out of the life God has in store for you.

But you don't have to settle. There is so much more beyond the walls! The passage in John 10:10 actually has great news after that solemn warning. After telling his followers about the thief, Jesus continues to tell them something better: "My purpose is to give them a rich and satisfying life."

In the context of this book, Jesus might have said, "The thief comes only to place you firmly behind a wall that will rob you of everything I have planned in your life. But I have come that you might have life—the life that's waiting after your Faith Breakthrough!"

If you were made for a breakthrough—for "a rich and satisfying life," as Jesus himself said—then that should happen naturally. You don't have to attain some great stature or learn some secret to enjoy it. You need only to tear down the walls that are keeping you from it. Like a healthy plant that has not grown beyond the confines of its pot, you may have walls that are keeping you stuck in a no-growth pattern that won't change until you address the problem.

I need to warn you right now, however, that there will be times in the pages ahead when you will be waiting for me to offer you an easy formula. I'll be very clear: I find no indication in the Bible that this is simple or easy. Instead, I find that it is *natural*. And because you were made to live life beyond the wall, I can assure you that it is absolutely worth it.

It's time for you to tear down the barriers that are holding you back. Now that you know how much is at stake, it is time to recognize just what you're up against. It's time to face the wall.

## DISCUSSION QUESTIONS

1. We live in a "quick fix" world that often tries to reduce problems to something less than they really are. For example, when people are in financial debt, some try to solve the problem by borrowing money—even though more money is not usually the heart of the problem. Can you think of an example of a problem that goes deeper than what people seem to be addressing?

2. Satan often offers enticing, but counterfeit, alternatives to God's best for our lives. What are the greatest temptations that people face today, and why do they seem so attractive?

3. Ryan talks about lies that can hold people back from the life God intended and gives several examples. How have commonly held "lies" kept you from what God has intended for your life?

4. Have you or someone you loved ever been robbed? How did that experience change the way you saw the world around you or how you behaved in the days that followed? Did you find that you had been robbed of something beyond the physical goods that were taken? If so, explain.

# chapter two

# WAKING UP TO A WALL

In a single night, a wall changed everything.

That August evening, even Berliners who were used to Germany's cool summer weather were surprised that the temperature had been so brisk. They hoped that the morning would bring a return to the beauty of the season.

On every level, it would not.

Men and women across Berlin woke up to find that every single street and bridge linking West Germany with East Germany had been closed down.

That day would come to be called "Barbed-Wire Sunday" for good reason. While Berlin slept, under the cover of darkness, construction began on the imposing barrier. Thousands of East German border police and dozens of Home Guard units, made up of thousands more troops, rushed to begin laying out 150 tons of barbed wire. Their carefully planned-out goal was to close every road and every bridge, cutting a great city literally in half. From that day on, the people of Berlin were haunted by a wall that held them back in more ways than we can imagine.[1]

There was, of course, the physical wall itself. More than two tons of staples were used to anchor the barbed-wire wall that was the first version of the Berlin Wall, and 18,200 concrete posts were poured. In all, they laid eighty-seven miles of razor wire in one night, trapping millions who, just one day earlier, had been able to come and go as they pleased.

But the wall wouldn't stay barbed wire. Beginning on August 15, the first of more than 45,000 separate reinforced concrete sections was poured. Each section of the wall would stand two inches short of twelve feet high—roughly as tall as the top of the backboards on a basketball court.

The East German guards replaced much of the barbed wire on top of the wall with a large, round pipe that was impossible to grip after they discovered that people would brave the terrible cuts of the razor wire to escape.

Beyond the towering presence being constructed before them, there was also a social wall. Many families lived just a few blocks from their relatives in Berlin. Tragically, these families woke up to discover they now lived on opposite sides of the wall. On that first day, Berliners could still see each other through the barbed-wire fence. Some of the most terrible pictures and film clips show family members standing as close as they dared to the menacing soldiers who lined the wall with machine guns unslung and at the ready. Many family members would catch sight of a loved one and would yell and wave at each other. The people on each side held up children and pets for their loved ones to see. They shouted words of encouragement that the wall would go down—that they would be together soon.

They were wrong.

It would be *a generation* before that wall came down.

And even deeper still, another wall went up in the hearts of many who fell victim to the separation that day. There was a tremendous emotional price to be paid in the lives of people on both sides of that fence. Dip into eyewitness accounts of Barbed-Wire Sunday and beyond, and you'll find deep evidence of emotional wounds and staggering wreckage.

Some eyewitnesses commented about the loss of access to a beautiful park or city building. Others poured out their hearts writing about the psychological wounds that came with the wall. Many experienced feelings of abandonment when not a single Western tank or soldier showed up to push back the wall or come to their aid, along with feelings of anger, fear, and a growing bitterness. There were rising sentiments of shock, grief, anger, confusion, and helplessness. The presence of these unseen emotions was every bit as real to them as the barrier dividing their city.

Whether the focus was on the physical, social, or emotional consequences for those who told the story, one theme remained consistent: the wall had robbed them of more than outsiders could completely comprehend.

Walls separate. They isolate. They cut us off from something . . . or from someone. East German leaders tried to offer the lie that the wall was for their protection from those in the West. But the Berliners knew the truth. The wall was there to blockade them from liberty, freedom, and hope. That is the nature of such walls.

## IT'S TIME TO WAKE UP AND FACE YOUR WALL

I've discovered in my years of ministry that the walls people face today are often invisible to the untrained eye but are every bit as real and imposing as the wall that went up in Berlin that infamous day.

*Walls separate. They isolate. They cut us off from something . . . or from someone.*

Every day wonderful, caring, loving, godly people like you and me wake up and find themselves facing life-choking, relationship-severing, legacy-altering, unseen walls. These walls are inescapable—we can't just close our eyes to make them go away. These are walls we must face and find a way to break through . . . or suffer the loss of freedom that will always plague us until we do.

In life, the unseen walls hurt us the most. Some difficulties—whether they are barriers, disabilities, trials, or economic hardships—are out in the open and cannot be ignored. Spiritual walls, on the other hand, can hinder progress, destroy families, and crush hope for years without anyone realizing exactly what is holding them back.

For me, the walls that came when my daughter Lily experienced a host of medical problems were more imposing than her multiple surgeries and hospital stays. The walls were built when I didn't know what to do with my nagging thoughts that this was not the way things were supposed to go. There was the overwhelming confusion of how God could allow this to happen to my child, the daunting sense of helplessness that left me feeling inadequate to rescue her, and the growing sense of fear that I might lose her.

Lily was only seven days old when we had to rush her back to the hospital because she was having trouble breathing. We were told she had a large hole in her heart called a ventricular septal defect. These birth defects come with varying degrees of severity, but the doctors informed us that we were dealing with a very delicate situation. Open-heart surgery was crucial, but if we went in too soon, Lily might not be strong enough to survive. On the other hand, if we waited too long, her already swollen and overworked heart could give out. So the mandate was to help her gain weight as quickly as possible in anticipation of an attempt to repair the hole—and, Lord willing, save her life.

When the heart doctor walked into Lily's hospital room that day, we were totally unprepared for the news. We had a precious week-old child who, while having given us a scare and an ambulance ride, gave all indications of being a healthy and happy baby. We were expecting to find out that she was still dealing with some fluids she had aspirated when she was born. They were running all sorts of tests to discern what was going on, and the only reason the cardiologist was even in the conversation was because a chest X-ray had indicated some extra fluid around her heart.

It so happened that our two older daughters were in the room with Lana and me when we got the diagnosis, and both sets of grandparents were visiting as well. One minute we were enjoying the conversation of family and the relief that Lily was safe and being closely monitored; the next moment we were told matter-of-factly that Lily had a much bigger problem, that our world would be put on hold for at least the next year, and that there was a delicate situation inside the tiny body of our baby girl. Even worse were the words left unspoken: We suddenly were not promised that we would get to keep her very long.

*I'm convinced that there is a whole new world awaiting those who are courageous enough to face their walls head-on, deal with them honestly, and take the steps toward a Faith Breakthrough.*

It was as if all the air had left the room. My wife's chest began to heave, as if she could not breathe. I wondered whether I was about to awaken from a horrible dream. We sat and listened to the details, the risks, the strategies, and the instructions in the way that only those who have been there can fully understand.

In a situation like this, the people around you somehow imagine that you can grasp all the details, and even dialogue about them, moments after the bomb has been dropped into your life. But while the voices continue with their unthinkable words, you're trying to wrestle with the instant emotions that are welling up in your heart. The disappointment. The questions of how this could have happened and how it might have been prevented. The anger at how it was shared. The determination to do whatever it takes to overcome. The tiny shred of hope that maybe they've made a mistake and that all will be well when the follow-up test is done.

I had been speaking on breakthroughs for several years by the time that doctor walked in, but suddenly those breakthroughs seemed as far away as the rejoicing that is supposed to come with the arrival of a child. Instead I could almost feel the walls going up around me.

Those same walls forced me to take a closer look at the truths of the Bible you'll read here, the truths that unlock the secret of the Faith Breakthrough. And those walls helped me understand how awesome it is when they finally come down.

I'm convinced that there is a whole new world awaiting those who are courageous enough to face their walls head-on, deal with them honestly, and take the steps toward a Faith Breakthrough. The process for bringing down these walls may not be easy, but it's worth it! You will take your wall seriously only when you fully understand what it's made of, so I will address that question in the next chapter.

## DISCUSSION QUESTIONS

1. Can you recall your earliest, or most vivid, memories of the Berlin Wall? What emotions did it stir in your heart? Why do you think it became such a symbol of oppression throughout the world?

2. Ryan shares some of the emotions he and his wife experienced during those critical moments after their daughter was diagnosed. Think back to some crisis moments in your own life. What were some of the first emotions you experienced? Did those emotions foreshadow any specific walls that later developed?

3. The Berlin Wall stood for an entire generation. Likewise, the walls in our lives generally last for many years. What makes them so difficult to tear down?

# chapter three

# DEFINING THE WALLS WE FACE

Whenever I share these concepts with a new group of people, I am always amazed how it seems so familiar to them. Their heads begin to nod, and their hearts resonate with the reality of unseen walls. Long before I give them any kind of definition, something deep within them already knows they are stuck. Still, it is important to clearly define the problem we are up against if we are ever to move beyond it to a life of Faith Breakthroughs. I define walls this way: a wall is an unhealthy mind-set that keeps you from living life as God intends.

Notice first what a wall is made of: it is composed of a mind-set—the frame of reference through which we process the world around us. Our belief systems literally "make up our minds" about what we see and experience. Notice also that a wall is not just any mind-set. It's an *unhealthy* one. In contrast, a healthy mind-set is focused on a sound set of convictions rather than emotions—helping us make choices based on the truth of Scripture. We've all seen books that promise we can change our lives by changing our emotions, as if all we have to do is have a brighter outlook on life. On the contrary, I know a lot of happy people whose happiness is based on false pretenses, happiness that will last only as long as the circumstances of life go well for them. But the Bible talks a great deal about the renewing of our minds. There is no doubt that many of our life choices, situations, and outcomes will be determined by the mind-sets that we program ourselves to live by. Consider Paul's words of wisdom in Romans 8:5-6:

> *A wall is an unhealthy mind-set that keeps you from living life as God intends.*

> Those who are dominated by the sinful nature think about sinful things, but those who are controlled by the Holy Spirit think about things that please the Spirit. So letting your sinful nature control your mind leads to death. But letting the Spirit control your mind leads to life and peace.

When we fail to trust what God has promised us, the situations in which we live can seem overwhelming and hopeless. Such a mind-set can bring the most optimistic people in the world to an absolute standstill.

You have probably heard the term *faith* all your life, but there's a good chance no one has really defined it for you.

Faith is believing God will do what he said he will do, regardless of timing or circumstances. Why is that important to understand? Because the strength of your mind-set will be directly related to the strength of your faith. In other words, when you stop believing that God will come through, your mind-set automatically begins to erode, and you will start building walls. Imagine that every negative thought toward what you're facing in life is a brick you are stacking, one on top of another, making your access to God's best for your life seem farther and farther away.

*Walls block us from living, giving, and experiencing God's best in our lives.*

Walls block us from living, giving, and experiencing God's best in our lives. He intends far more for us than we will ever experience until we break through our walls. Additionally, because walls are built based on our attitudinal outlook, we may confuse what we are seeing with what is really the problem. That is why it's also important to understand the most common areas of confusion regarding walls.

## WHAT WALLS ARE *NOT*

In April 1986, Geraldo Rivera hosted a television special that had become one of the most anticipated events in media history. *The Mystery of Al Capone's Vault* was the most-watched syndicated special to date, with more than 30 million viewers. As the title hinted, Rivera was to open a hidden safe that had been owned by Capone and that had remained closed since the 1930s. It was rumored to hold untold secret treasures—or even a dead body.

After all of the hype and expectation, however, the opening of the safe itself turned out to be a colossal letdown. The only things the vault held were several empty, dirty bottles and debris. For years afterward, "Al Capone's Vault" was used to express the idea of a heavily anticipated event that failed to live up to its hype.

Unlike the efforts to penetrate that safe, we can be sure there is treasure on the other side of the wall; but far too often our efforts go to empty pursuits. With all that's at stake as you begin the journey past your walls, it would be a shame to focus all your energy on something that wasn't the problem in the first place.

The concept of walls may not be a new one, but there is often a misunderstanding of exactly which walls we are able to overcome and which walls we should care about overcoming in the first place.

There are three major misconceptions about walls that commonly throw people off the track of their breakthroughs. Recognizing these misconceptions up front can save us years of wasted energy:

### Walls are not our circumstances.

I've reminded my congregation many times of this important fact. Each time I teach Faith Breakthroughs at a conference or seminar across the country, I try to make it very clear that the walls those in attendance are facing are not the problems themselves.

If our walls were our circumstances, then we could simply say, "That husband of mine is my wall!" or "My illness is my wall!" We could blame the board of directors that didn't accept us or the prodigal child who hurt us or the political system that robbed us. But none of those situations is the substance of a spiritual wall.

From the very beginning of time, humankind has been looking for excuses in their circumstances rather than pointing to the real wall. When Adam blamed Eve, he said in essence, "Lord, it's that woman you gave me! She gave me the fruit, and I ate it! And now all the good stuff is back behind a wall!" (Genesis 3:12, my paraphrase).

If circumstances can be walls, then the apostle Paul lists what could be considered a parade of walls in 2 Corinthians 11:24-28:

> *Five different times* the Jewish leaders gave me *thirty-nine lashes. Three times* I was *beaten* with rods. *Once* I was *stoned. Three times* I was *shipwrecked. Once* I spent a whole night and a day *adrift at sea.* I have traveled on *many long journeys.* I have *faced danger* from rivers and from robbers. I have *faced danger* from my own people, the Jews, as well as from the Gentiles. I have *faced danger* in the cities, in the deserts, and on the seas. And I have *faced danger* from men who claim to be believers but are not. I have worked hard and long, enduring *many sleepless nights.* I have been *hungry and thirsty* and have often gone without food. I have shivered in the *cold, without enough clothing* to keep me warm. Then, besides all this, I have the daily burden of my *concern for all the churches.* (Emphasis added)

If you're counting, that's the memory of more than twenty negative circumstances—any one of which would stand to hold Paul back from abundant living if walls were all about circumstances.

But listen to the apostle's words: "I want you to know, my dear brothers and sisters, that everything that has happened to me here has helped to spread the Good News" (Philippians 1:12).

He was not looking at circumstances as walls. He was seeing circumstances—even negative ones—as doorways to move *past* walls. That's a mind-set that happens only when we focus on the one who has power over any circumstances: God. Paul saw the challenges he faced as catalysts for good and gain, in his life and in the lives of others. In fact, he weighed in again on circumstances not being walls later on, saying:

> Not that I was ever in need, for I have learned how
> to be content with whatever I have. I know how
> to live on almost nothing or with everything. I
> have learned the secret of living in every situation,
> whether it is with a full stomach or empty, with
> plenty or little. (Philippians 4:11-12)

If you're going through an especially difficult time in your life, it might sound offensive to say that your circumstances aren't your problem. My point here is not to minimize the challenges you face in life, but it is intended to take your eyes off those events and place them on something you can really address. The problem with identifying your circumstances as your walls is that you often have no power to change them.

On the other hand, when we address the walls of unhealthy mind-sets in our lives, the circumstances—and how we view them—often improve as well over time.

In fact, we should never assume that God cannot or will not change our circumstances. As our walls come down because our faith has increased, we have every reason to anticipate that God will do things that only he can do in our midst! I firmly believe, and have personally witnessed, that God can work miracles in the midst of dire circumstances. The difference is that we cannot change them on our own.

*We need not depend on the circumstances to change in order to experience a Faith Breakthrough.*

That, then, is the first thing that walls are not. Walls are not our circumstances. We need not depend on the circumstances to change in order to experience a Faith Breakthrough.

### Walls are not just bad feelings.

When you begin to break through the walls in your life, there's a very strong chance that you are going to experience great joy and satisfaction. Likewise, some of the feelings you experience are a direct result of the walls you face. However, feelings are not the best barometers of breakthroughs.

Consider the letter to the Ephesians in Scripture, in which Paul challenges the people not to live according to their feelings:

> With the Lord's authority I say this: Live no longer
> as the Gentiles do, for they are hopelessly confused.
> Their minds are full of darkness; they wander far

from the life God gives because they have closed
their minds and hardened their hearts against him.
They have no sense of shame. They live for lustful
pleasure and eagerly practice every kind of impurity.
(Ephesians 4:17-19)

The people described in this passage fell into the trap of
thinking their emotions should guide their every decision,
but their emotions led them down a path that made them
"hopelessly confused."

Our mind-sets are not the same as our feelings. A mind-
set is a way of seeing life based on a set of beliefs. Feelings are
ways of reacting to our surroundings based on our emotions.
We can have one feeling and choose an altogether different
mind-set.

This becomes important in recognizing that not all negative feelings are unhealthy mind-sets that need to change.
God gave us our emotions, but that doesn't mean we should
always follow them. I run into people all the time who need
to make major changes in their lives but resist those changes
because they involve too much discomfort. In fact, it's common for such people to blame God for their unwillingness
to move forward. They say things like, "I just don't feel led
to do anything about it right now," or, "I have a real peace
about what I'm already doing." But feelings that are based on
something contrary to God's best for us are just cop-outs.

*Walls are not protective boundaries.*
This myth is often an offshoot of the "feelings" misconcep-
tion described a moment ago. Since the beginning of time,

people have avoided needed self-discipline or healthy habits in the name of discomfort. But boundaries are good for us, regardless of how they make us feel.

Several years ago an interesting study was conducted on the playground behavior of young schoolchildren, and the way they responded to various boundaries. The children came from several different schools, each one judged to have essentially the same-size play area. The students were from areas comparable in socioeconomic status, and the classes had roughly the same ratio of teachers to students. Yet there was one major difference between the two types of schools being studied: one group offered children a fenced playground; the other group had no fence around their playground.

When the study was over, the students with the clearly marked boundary showed the most cooperative play, had fewer playground fights, and exhibited lower levels of anxiety during recess.

When it comes to playground behavior, children playing inside a fence experienced an inner security that other children did not. The same applies to boundaries in our lives, and this security and self-discipline should not be confused with the detrimental walls that blockade us from good things.

Obviously, the top athletes in the world have made sacrifices to be at the top of their games. To be the best, they must have very clear boundaries related to diet, exercise, practice, and more. First Corinthians 9:25-27 compares the victorious life of a Christ-follower to these intentional boundaries:

All athletes are disciplined in their training. They
do it to win a prize that will fade away, but we do it

for an eternal prize. So I run with purpose in every step. I am not just shadowboxing. I discipline my body like an athlete, training it to do what it should. Otherwise, I fear that after preaching to others I myself might be disqualified.

While freedom-loving Americans may bristle at the idea that limits are good for us, it's true. In fact, this incredible passage even supports a desire for withholding some pleasure in order to attain something later on. We have to stay inside the lines God has set if we want to get to our destination safely. To keep our mind-sets and actions inside the boundaries of God's Word doesn't limit us but frees us to experience life at its best.

That's because boundaries are not our walls.

I love the game of basketball, and I have played thousands of games between high school, college, and pickup games at the park and in the driveway. But I cannot think of a single game I played in with no lines. The game of basketball takes place inside boundaries. And while that might seem restrictive, it actually spells freedom to a player, and it clearly spells out positive limits. I've been in many games where there was disagreement as to whether someone went out-of-bounds, but I've never seen anyone argue that the boundaries shouldn't be there.

I have a friend who grew up with his mother in a single-parent home. When he was in junior high, his mother had to have major surgery, and his least favorite aunt came to live with them to help out.

She was his least favorite aunt because she brought with

her a number of rules that seemed incredibly restrictive. Things like going to bed at a reasonable time of night, having to do homework before watching television, or eating dinner before dessert. These new boundaries seemed unreasonable, unnecessary, and unloving, at least in his eyes at the time.

Today, because she helped to instill structure and appropriate boundaries in his life, he refers to that same woman as his favorite aunt. Like a strict aunt who establishes rules that sometimes seem inconvenient, the boundaries in our lives can be our greatest allies in the quest for a Faith Breakthrough. Positive boundaries in life have nothing to do with the kind of walls that keep us from God's best. In fact, a lack of boundaries can lead to many walls. Walls rob us of progress and cut us off from life. Legitimate boundaries bring clarity and structure to our lives. Boundaries add; walls take away. Boundaries ring true over time. Walls get worse each day. It is essential for us to know the difference.

## DEFINING THE REAL WALL

The Gospel of Mark captures an incredible scene of breaking through walls and helps us better understand how walls are defined—and how they are often confused. If we could have been there, we'd have found Jesus teaching in a house that was completely packed with an attentive audience. People were wedged into every square inch of sitting or standing room inside, while a growing crowd spilled out the front door and onto the entryway and yard, each one trying to catch a glimpse of, and to hear a word from, Jesus.

Ken Gire describes the crowd as "a catch-all collection

of seekers, spectators, and spies. Some came with a hopeful eye, to be healed. Others came with a curious eye, to be convinced. Still others came with a jaundiced eye. To find out who was rocking the religious boat and to stop him from making any more waves."[2]

It was the people who were late to the party whom the apostle Mark most clearly described: four men and a paralytic. Just hearing the word *paralytic* conjures up images of incredible challenges for the one who has to carry that label in our day. In Jesus' day, it meant facing tremendous challenges just to survive.

This man's entire life had been pressed into the space of a three-foot-by-six-foot mat. Never being able to turn on his side, leave his home without help, or perhaps even reach out for another's hand. This paralytic lived in Capernaum, which meant that, from the house where Jesus sat, it would have been only a short walk to the beautiful Sea of Galilee— yet this man could never take the first step toward the thin, sandy beach on his own.

There were no steps. There was no privacy. He had to rely on others for everything.

He would have to be moved and turned often to try to keep the inevitable mat sores from becoming too inflamed or infected. And of course, he would have faced the humiliation of being cleaned and bathed after every bodily function.

Think about how challenging that would have been. Those physical circumstances, however, were not his walls. Remember that walls are not our circumstances—even circumstances as dire as this man's. But we can certainly understand how such circumstances might lead him to a host of walls to overcome. His physical paralysis brought confinement. And because he was a person designed for movement, we can easily imagine the inevitable frustrations of having to wait for things around him to be moved, or someone to move something for him. And most likely there was loneliness. Boredom. Shame. Sorrow. Anger at God. Disappointment at opportunities lost. Now, those are mind-sets that can be built into walls.

But for all he had lost, there was something that added immensely to this man's life. *Friends.* The four who were willing to carry him to Jesus. Perhaps they had been there when their friend's body was broken by accident or injury. We're not told that he'd been a paralytic all his life, as others in the Bible were described. Perhaps these same friends who were caring for his needs had been there when he'd lost use of his limbs. All we know for sure is that on this day, they were the ones carrying him to see Jesus. And they were also the ones who ran right into total disappointment when they saw the crowd spilling outside the house.

### A desperate plan . . .

We're also not told how these four initially handled the disappointment they must have felt. When their goal of getting their friend to Jesus was blocked, it had to be a letdown. Nor are we let in on the despair that the paralytic might have felt when he realized that his best chance for being healed wasn't going to happen. There was simply no way any of them were going to get into that house with the press of bodies in front of them. And certainly no one was willing to give up his place inside.

We're left to wonder which one of the paralytic's friends

first came up with the outside-the-box idea to use the outside staircase, but we can almost picture the look crossing all four sets of eyes when the suggestion was first made.

Perhaps after it was spoken there was an initial feeling of doubt, but as the thought sank in, it turned from *No way!* to *Yes, that might work!* However it happened, they had a new glimmer of hope for their friend.

Perhaps they could get to Jesus after all!

All they needed to do was carry their friend up the outside stairs to the top of the roof. That wasn't a problem. They had one friend for each mat corner. The problem was, as Jews, all their lives they had been taught not to interrupt a rabbi while he was teaching. And surely they would know that the people below them would soon be bellowing with shock and anger when the tiles and dust came pouring down into the room where Jesus sat.

But none of that mattered to these four friends.

They knew they had found a way to get their friend in front of the Healer. After all, this was the same person who had tossed a demon out of a man in another city. The same one who had healed a leper in another nearby town. Surely the terrible circumstances that their friend faced could be relieved if he could just come before Jesus.

It was their faces that Jesus would have seen first, peering down from above when the dust clouds cleared. Faces with faith written all over them. Jesus saw a faith that refused to surrender to the situation—a faith that moved aside a rooftop. He was touched with compassion for their friend.

Then something amazing happened.

Because Jesus is God, he looked at the circumstances.

Here was this broken body before him, but Jesus was looking beyond what everyone else saw as the problem and saw an invisible wall that was far more essential to address. Jesus was able to look into this man's soul and see an unseen wall raised up by sin and shame.

That's when Jesus said to the man who was paralyzed, "My child, your sins are forgiven" (Mark 2:5).

That man had been physically washed by others countless times, and always there was the need for another cleansing. But then Jesus' words, "Your sins are forgiven," washed over him and joined the tears washing down the sides of his face. At the very deepest level of his heart and soul (can you imagine!) his life *right then* was being washed clean of sin and shame by his Creator!

The freedom! No guilt! No shame!

He was becoming new from the inside out. This man's faults had been no less real because his physical actions were limited to that three-foot-by-six-foot mat. This paralyzed man was likely just as happy to be free of sin as the most mobile of sinners was free to carouse about that ancient city.

Jesus' words lifted off the crushing inner weight of a Wall of Doubt or Anger or Rebellion that no one else in the room could see: an unseen but very real wall that Jesus knew was really cutting him off from life and from his heavenly Father.

But there were those in the room who, when they heard Jesus' words, were ready to curse his claim to tear down the unseen wall, though none inside dared to speak his sentiments out loud. The religious leaders all around Jesus were whispering to themselves, "This man has just claimed the power of

God for himself! *Only God can forgive sins!* Only God himself can tear down that kind of wall!" (Mark 2:7, paraphrased).

And Jesus, sensing the hatred in their hearts, said to them, "Why do you question this in your hearts? Is it easier to say to the paralyzed man 'Your sins are forgiven,' or 'Stand up, pick up your mat, and walk'?" (Mark 2:8-9).

The simple answer might be that both are *impossible*. That is, of course, unless you're God. And to sweep out all the hateful feelings that had filled the room and replace them with joy and amazement, Jesus did something truly amazing: "[He said,] 'So I will prove to you that the Son of Man has the authority on earth to forgive sins.' Then Jesus turned to the paralyzed man and said, 'Stand up, pick up your mat, and go home!'" (Mark 2:10-11).

And the man did. A man who had lived with the most terrible of physical barriers now stood up and walked away for all to see. Even more amazing, he was free of his spiritual and emotional walls as well.

It's important to note that God changed the invisible walls before he addressed the physical circumstances. The physical circumstances don't always change, but the spiritual walls can never withstand the power of God's Word.

If we could have been there, I'm sure we would have seen five friends dancing and crying and praising God as they walked down to the beach, with the paralytic carrying his mat above his head. . . .

For walls seen and unseen had come down.

It works the same in your life and mine. We focus on what we can see, but the unseen walls are just as real as the physical barriers we face.

Walls separate. Walls isolate. Walls intimidate. But walls are no match for God.

That's why it's so important to understand that the invisible walls are there. They don't have to dominate or define you any longer! Just like this paralyzed man, you have to get to the heart of the problem. The wall in your life may be something you have never really thought about before, but it is a reality you cannot afford to ignore. Beyond it lies what you've been waiting for.

By now you know what walls are and what they are not. You have a glimpse of what can be when the walls come down. But perhaps there is still the temptation to shrug off the significance of the walls in your life.

It's time to expose the truth about the danger of walls.

## DISCUSSION QUESTIONS

1.  Do you know people who have become so fixated on circumstances that could not be changed that they missed out on many other blessings? Based on what you have read, what is wrong with seeing our circumstances as walls?

2.  Ryan has made it clear that walls are made of unhealthy mindsets, but he also says that walls are not emotions. What is the difference between a mind-set and emotion? Is it possible for a person to have a mind-set that doesn't reflect his or her emotional feelings? Why or why not?

3.  Think back to the story of Jesus' healing the paralytic in Mark 2. On a scale of 1 to 10, with 10 being completely satisfied, how satisfied do you think you would have been if

you had been there and seen Jesus forgive the man's sin, not realizing that he soon would heal the man physically as well? Why do we tend to look only at the outward circumstances while God is far more interested in our hearts? What are the benefits of looking at our hearts through God's eyes?

# chapter four

# THE HIGH COST OF WALLS

I have to be honest with you: if it were up to me, this chapter would be full of simple ideas on how to overcome the wall you're facing. But if I did that now, you would not appreciate just how significant a step it's going to be to experience the breakthrough in store for you.

I recently purchased a book that promised to lead to a flat stomach with a few simple changes to my eating habits. On the other hand, it also promised that I could eat all the fast food I wanted! Now that sounded too good to be true . . . and it was. Two weeks later I was off the diet after *gaining* a few pounds. In its place, I simply started to eat smarter and make sacrifices. Only then did the pounds come off. The truth is I prefer to eat whatever has the most flavor—and to eat lots of it. But even more important was my desire to avoid the consequences that come with poor choices. I didn't want to deal with all the health factors that often accompany overeating. I had too much to live for.

Think of this book like a nutritional plan for your mind and spirit. There will be no progress without right choices, and those right choices rarely come until you fully comprehend the danger of the alternative.

## POISONOUS WALLS

My family moved to Central Texas when I was five years old. I remember becoming fast friends with Brian, the boy next door. We spent hours outside playing cowboys and Indians, cops and robbers, and every other game that comes naturally to little boys. One day soon after my family had settled into our new home, we were playing in the front yard when Brian noticed a snake in the bushes. Of course, avid hunters as we were, we immediately determined that the snake must be captured. We found an old pickle jar in Brian's garage and were ready to go.

The plan was simple: I would distract the snake from the front, and Brian would sneak up behind and grab it. Once he threw it in the jar, I would quickly screw on the lid. Within five minutes, we had corralled the snake into its new home without incident.

To our surprise, however, when the snake was caught in the jar, it didn't go down easily. It began frantically striking at the glass. It was such a curious thing that I went into the house to show my father. But when he saw our trophy, he turned white as a sheet and quickly grabbed the jar. *What's the big deal, Dad? It's just a snake!*

Coming from out of state, I was unfamiliar with the wildlife of the region. It turns out that every poisonous snake found in North America resides in Texas—including the western diamondback rattlesnake. And my buddy Brian and I had captured one for our very own, one of the deadliest snakes in the world!

It wasn't until that moment that I realized I had been playing with my life. And my dad made sure I never forgot that the threat doesn't diminish just because you're unaware of the danger. Snakes kill unsuspecting five-year-olds, too.

When it comes to the spiritual walls that every person confronts, there is a danger that is often overlooked, and the threat of walls in our lives is either ignored or greatly underestimated. In fact, walls can be even worse than snakebites, because when someone is bitten, at least he or she knows it right away and can seek medical attention. Spiritual walls creep in slowly. They masquerade as reasonable structures. And then, while we don't even realize it, they grow so high that they rob us of the life that God intends us to live, a life of faith in him.

There is a treasure of joy awaiting us on the other side of our walls—the rewarding lives for which we were created. And if walls can keep us from those blessings, then that's just fine to the enemy of the breakthrough. After all, his primary goal is not only to keep us from blessings. It is to keep us from the God of those blessings. Our enemy knows that the privilege of knowing God and walking with him is the greatest blessing of all, but he'd love to keep us distracted from that wonderful truth.

I've seen too many people fall for the con of the wall-defined life: the lie that there's nothing for us beyond where we find ourselves now.

A member of my church who grew up behind the Iron Curtain in Germany shared a story with me about what life was like in the former Soviet Union. He said that the government was constantly putting out propaganda to the people behind the Berlin Wall to lie about life on the other side, creating the illusion of devastation, corruption, and even torture. Most of the people in Berlin, however, knew the truth anyway because of a secret source: many of them kept in touch with the West through radio and television channels that were accessible on their side. But there were some who missed out on the truthful broadcasts.

My friend Ulrich related to me that there was a certain region down in a valley whose geography kept its inhabitants from picking up the promises and hopes of a better life awaiting them on the other side of the Wall. He said that this area became known as "The Valley of the Clueless."

How many people are living in the spiritual equivalent of this valley today, having totally forgotten, or missed, the promise of something better? My friend, I wish I could look you in the eye as I tell you that I've personally seen what happens when the walls come down. Walls have been broken for others, and they can be broken for you!

You don't have to settle for life as it has been, whether resentment, discouragement, shame, or something else holds you back. This book will lead you to everything you need to break through your walls, but first you must determine that you will no longer stand for the walls in your life—not a single day longer. You must see the walls for what they truly are.

## *Walls never satisfy.*

We often get a false sense of security when Walls of Doubt or Fear go up in our lives—as if these walls were actually protecting us from something we could not handle. However, no matter how much comfort they may bring, the walls are a poor substitute for what can be—the freedom in which we are intended to live.

When I was in college, a group of guys I was traveling with came through Chicago. We knew we needed to stop for the night somewhere, but as only a carefree single student could appreciate, we showed up with no hotel reservations and very little funding. Thinking we could just talk our way into getting a room on a busy weekend, we walked into the lobby of the Westin, one of the finest hotels in downtown Chicago. Of course, the first thing the clerk at the reservation desk told us was that they were all booked up. But as we persisted and used all our charm, she finally relented and said that—amazingly—she had found something for us. In fact, she had found a suite large enough for all of us to stay in one room, and at an incredibly low price!

Almost swaggering with our ability to negotiate a great room and rate, my friends and I walked through the expensive lobby, piled into the impressive brass-and-wood-lined elevator, and off we went to one of the highest floors. When we arrived at the door to our room, just above the number were the words *Presidential Suite*. And just when things couldn't have gotten any better, we opened the door to our room. Not only was the suite huge, with an incredible view of downtown Chicago, there was a grand piano, a pool table, and two huge televisions.

What wasn't to love about all the games and distractions around us? Except, of course, one thing . . .

The reason we were given the room, and at such a discount, was that our suite had *no bedrooms*. It was actually the huge main room in between two sets of bedrooms, one on each side. However, those bedrooms had been locked off and were rented to other guests.

It really was fine by us for the first few hours. We had a huge room with plenty of distractions, electronics, and games. That is, no one cared until we finally grew tired of playing pool and using all the other amenities and wanted to lie down and rest. That is when it really sank in that there was no place to truly rest in that room.

In many ways, that is a clear picture of what walls do in our lives. We were just one wall away from a room designed specifically for the rest and refreshment we so desperately wanted. But those beds might as well have been miles from where we were standing. As the night wore on, it made less and less difference that we were on a high floor, or in a suite, or surrounded by expensive toys. There was no rest.

When we keep walls up in our lives, we can distract ourselves with all the toys and gadgets we want, but we are blocking ourselves from ever being able to truly lay our hurt and pain down and find God's rest.

If you're worn out, body and soul; if you go to work in the morning and all you can think about is making it through the day; if you lie down at night thinking that life has left you behind, chances are good that you're living behind a wall, a wall that needs to come down today. But a lack of genuine rest is not the only problem with leaving walls standing in your life.

## Walls always get worse.

You may already have a wall in mind that has become part of your everyday existence. And you may already have convinced yourself that this wall is really not so bad. Before you decide that the process of getting past the wall is just too much trouble, keep this in mind: your wall will not stay the same. The truth is, walls always get worse.

Every family should have the opportunity to visit our nation's capital. While on my family's first visit to Washington, DC, I took our girls to see my favorite monument. I've always been impressed with the beautiful architecture of the Thomas Jefferson Memorial and with Jefferson's legacy of achievements. Since our oldest daughter, Ryley, was about five at the time, I felt like she was old enough to truly appreciate this glorious structure with me for the first time, and so we went on ahead of the rest of the family.

As we walked inside, we took in the massive, nineteen-foot-tall statue of our third president and the ornate writings surrounding the rotunda. Ryley was totally transfixed by the size of the sculpture itself, but I went around the room surrounding Jefferson's likeness, pointing out key phrases carved in stone and doing my best to impart to her the importance of what those words mean to our country. After all, this was the man who had written the Declaration of Independence!

When I had finally finished my enthusiastic and motivating

speech on Jefferson, I could tell by the look on Ryley's face that she was less than impressed with everything I had said.

"And besides that, Dad," she proclaimed, "he was really big!"

The entire time I was walking her around the memorial, talking about all of Jefferson's achievements, Ryley was mesmerized by only one thing: the size of this man!

I was wrapped up in all that Jefferson had done. She was wrapped up in staring at the huge statue in front of her.

Thomas Jefferson was actually very tall. At six-foot-two, he was considered way above average height, which was five-foot-six at the time. But while Jefferson was tall, every description of him says "tall and thin." That's not how his statue is carved. It's a bronze behemoth. It's designed to be larger than life. And so, too, are the walls that remain in our lives. They will inevitably grow higher and wider and heavier every day, taking up more and more of our emotional and spiritual breathing space, commanding more and more of our focus in the process.

Perhaps one way to understand the dynamic, rather than static, nature of walls is to switch the metaphor for a moment and put them in the context of a cancer. I have a friend who runs one of the top genetics institutes focused on curing cancer. One day I asked him for information on a person I knew who had been told he had a fast-growing cancer. The cancer expert gently explained that the term *fast-growing* was not technically accurate. He went on to say that when cancerous masses seem to grow quickly, it is not because the cells themselves speed up and divide more quickly than other cells; it's just that cancer cells never stop dividing. Healthy cells have special instructions in their DNA that tell them when to quit multiplying. Cancer cells have lost or, for whatever reason (still unknown), chosen to ignore those "stop dividing" instructions. So a fast-spreading cancer is one that just keeps on dividing and refuses to stop pushing important things out of the way as it grows.

What's true with cancer is also true with walls. They continue to grow. And at the same time these unhealthy mind-sets grow worse, they decrease our willingness to admit they are there.

### *Walls cause us to fake fulfillment.*

Walls can separate us from lots of blessings that God has in store, but perhaps none of the blockades are felt more universally than the separations felt at home. Regardless of which wall you're facing, there is a strong possibility that it has impacted your family life. That's because walls keep genuine faith from playing its rightful role in the most personal of our priorities.

In the first decade of the twenty-first century, we witnessed an alarming exodus of Americans from churches nationwide. People are frustrated with the disconnect they see between their faith and their real lives. A significantly decreasing number of Americans are participating in the most basic Christian practice: the weekly gathering for worship, teaching, prayer, and fellowship.[3] Adults of all ages are finding that their faith traditions have failed them, or at least have left them bored and uninterested. It might simply be a trend if we could also state that these de-churched masses were headed home to carry out their faith walks on a more personal level, that the only thing that was failing was the formality of meeting together in large gatherings. But faith isn't going home! Few would argue with the fact that the American family is also reaching all-time lows in many categories.

Broken relationships.

Severed generations.

Rampant immorality.

It's a troubling cycle: Faith becomes too formalized and less personal; the church looks—and we feel—hypocritical for faking it week after week; we slowly drift away from church attendance, or we get better at shielding our authentic lives (the ones lived out at home) from the lives we reveal to others on Sunday. Our faith at home erodes as we try to balance these two selves, so we construct a set of false realities (mind-sets) that will shield us from admitting that things aren't working. These false realities can sound innocent enough:

- "God helps those who help themselves." If I keep working hard and trying to do what's right, my marriage and my children will turn out okay.
- In the real world, there's no time to invest in spiritual things. I'll deal with that stuff when I'm older.

And worse, our children can't help but notice the hypocrisy, and their walls go up as well:

- I hear about God at church, but I don't see God really changing my family.
- If that's what faith is, then you can have it, Mom and Dad.

We try to compensate by making church life more formulaic and less personal—as if all God has offered us is a list of instructions rather than the gift of his presence and participation in our lives.

The cycle continues until we're left with defeated lives, broken homes, and empty faith. After two decades of ministry, I believe this is the heart of the problem: there is a disconnect—a wall—between what many people know of Jesus at church and the Jesus they really know at home.

This separation affects everyone, whether home is in a college dormitory or a nursing facility. And I am absolutely convinced that until these walls come down in our lives, and *at home*, the church doesn't have a chance at turning the tide.

We hear much today about the "missional church." It's an exploding movement that urges people to move their faith outside of the church building and into their communities. That is an important cause, but if we ignore the walls standing in our own homes, our testimonies will be artificial and contrived. Eventually, the people around us will question our words as they see that huge gap between faith and home. We must understand and break down the walls we face by allowing Faith Breakthroughs to permeate every aspect of our lives.

### Walls teach us to settle for less than God's best.

The longer we let walls stand, the more likely we are to focus on what led to the wall in the first place and to forget all about what we're missing on the other side. The longer we let walls stand, the more they will erase our belief in things miraculous, which is never a good thing to do with a miracle-working God.

You begin to doubt that the wall can ever come down.

Anytime you stop expecting something beyond your current situation, you begin to settle for far less than what could be. I've run into many people who have made the disappointing decision to simply set up camp on the wrong side of the wall and call it a life.

*Anytime you stop expecting something beyond your current situation, you begin to settle for far less than what could be.*

In his landmark book *The Search for Significance*, Robert S. McGee spoke of the false beliefs that can keep us from living an abundant life. One of those is the belief that "I am what I am. I cannot change. I am hopeless." This is the belief that creeps in when we give up on our breakthroughs.

In his book, McGee tells about counseling a man named Jeff, who had given up hope of ever changing. McGee wrote, "I explained to Jeff that he needed a new perspective, not just new efforts based on his old, pessimistic attitude. He needed to develop a new self-concept based on the unconditional love and acceptance of God. Both Jeff's past failures and God's unconditional love were realities, but the question was which one Jeff would value more."

It is easy to picture the man McGee was speaking to having settled for what he thought was the only life available, a life behind a Wall of Shame. And if we choose to dwell on the realities that built our walls in the first place, we will settle as well. Even worse, the longer we settle in, the more resigned we become to the idea that this must be our lot in life.

*Walls can outlive our opportunities.*

Contrary to prevailing sentiment, you don't have an indefinite period of time to overcome your walls. Life is full of built-in deadlines, some of which are known and some that remain mysteries until it's too late. That's what makes addressing walls now so very important.

My wife's grandparents were some of the most generous people I have ever known, but they also knew how to make a dollar last. Like many of the Greatest Generation, they grew up during the Great Depression.

People who grew up in the breadline days of the Great Depression learned to scrimp, save, water things down, and do all they could to make what little they had go as far as it could. Like many who came out of that experience of having so little, Lana's grandparents were extremely frugal throughout the rest of their lives.

I came face-to-face with that hard-earned tendency to stretch things out as far as possible when Lana and I were staying at their house several years ago. I'm a breakfast eater, so when we all got up, I looked forward to a big bowl of cereal. While I love milk, I'll admit—and my mother will testify—that I'm adamant (phobic?) about milk being ice-cold and fresh enough to not be even *remotely* close to the carton's expiration date. Have you seen that guy at the grocery store who reaches to the very back of the milk cooler to get the milk that was just unloaded off the truck? That guy is me.

So of course, before putting the milk on my cereal, I stopped to examine the expiration date—and nearly dropped the carton!

The milk wasn't just *near* the expiration date; it was three months *past* the date on the carton! To me, that put it in the nuclear waste category.

"PawPaw," I said in shock, "do you realize that your milk is three months old?" And that's when he told me how they liked to stock up on things when they found them at closeout prices at the store, a habit they'd formed in—you guessed it—the Great Depression.

It seems they'd loaded up on milk several months before when it was on sale, and thawed a carton for our breakfast. But there was a big problem. PawPaw wasn't sure exactly when they'd thawed out the milk, nor was he sure how long frozen milk could last.

Meaning that there was an expiration date, but *nobody knew when it was coming*!

As you might imagine, there was no cereal for me that morning. When there's no knowledge of the expiration date, you can never be sure when everything will go sour.

And that's why you cannot wait another day to start the journey beyond your wall.

Ephesians 5:16 puts it this way: "Make the most of every opportunity in these evil days." The Bible is reminding us once again of this sobering principle that ought to demonstrate the urgency of each moment we are given: life is full of expiration dates.

We never know when the wall might become too exhausting or too overwhelming or simply too normal for us to care anymore. There is too much of life at stake to put off a breakthrough.

## WHEN INVISIBLE WALLS HELD BACK A NATION

Do you know anyone who has named a son *Shaphat*? What about *Geuel*? Most likely you don't (that is, if you mostly hang around loving parents). But what about the names Joshua or Caleb? It's very likely that there's a Joshua or Caleb in your school or family. In fact, in a recent list of the top 100 boys' names in the United States, Caleb was number 31 and Joshua came in at 6. Shaphat and Geuel apparently fell short of the list.

Why not Shaphat or Geuel? After all, these men, like Joshua and Caleb, were part of a handpicked group of spies sent out by Moses to peek into the Promised Land before God's people moved in. They were part of an elite group of twelve spies, one man from each of the twelve tribes of Israel. But no one (unless they're *really* good at Bible trivia) can name a single one of the ten besides Joshua and Caleb. Why? In part, because of walls.

Ten spies who went into the Promised Land saw walls, not an opportunity to trust God's Word and provision. In fact, the more time they spent observing this land's inhabitants, fortified dwelling places, and the giants who lived there, the more doubt, fear, and unbelief came into their hearts. And as we already know from our earlier definition of walls, the more we allow unhealthy mind-sets to direct our decisions, the higher our walls will grow.

Keep in mind, before the spies were sent out, each one of them knew that almighty God had said that this land was to be their land—hence the term *Promised Land*. But bad mind-sets have a terrible way of tearing down promises and raising up walls.

Watch the way these walls grew when Moses called for the spies to make their report. Moses commanded each of the spies to "see what the land is like, and find out whether the people living there are strong or weak, few or many" (Numbers 13:18).

All twelve spies reported back accurately regarding the first part of Moses' questions. Indeed, the Promised Land was "a land flowing with milk and honey" (Numbers 13:27). In other words, the land was incredible.

But so ended ten of the spies' attempts at accuracy in reporting. For when it came to the state of the enemy they would face, the report that ten brought back was anything but reality based. Reality stopped when the ten started listing all the tribes they must face if they were to cross the Jordan River and claim their Land of Promise:

> But the people living there are powerful, and their towns are large and fortified. We even saw giants there, the descendants of Anak! The Amalekites live in the Negev, and the Hittites, Jebusites, and Amorites live in the hill country. The Canaanites live along the coast of the Mediterranean Sea and along the Jordan Valley. (Numbers 13:28-29)

That's like going down the list of names on a visiting team's program before the game starts and seeing stats like, "Mark Smith, 6' 5", 380 pounds; Bill Davis, 6' 9", 345 pounds"—and those are just the water boys! Most people know that there can be some inflation of actual players' heights and weights in sports. But what the ten spies reported was like listing the opposing team as being so big and so terrifying it causes the whole team to break into near hysteria.

That's when Caleb (number 31 on the Top 100 Names chart, number one in terms of trusting God's promises) spoke up: "But Caleb tried to quiet the people as they stood before Moses. 'Let's go at once to take the land,' he said. 'We can certainly conquer it!'" (Numbers 13:30).

Caleb had seen the exact same challenges as the other ten spies, but he came back believing God's promises, not seeing walls. As the story continued to unfold, it is amazing to see how fear and doubt started growing walls for ten of the other spies from life-size to "Dad . . . he was *really* big!" size. "But the other men who had explored the land with him disagreed. 'We can't go up against them! They are stronger than we are!' So they spread this bad report about the land among the Israelites: 'The land we traveled through and explored will devour anyone who goes to live there. All the people we saw were huge. We even saw giants there'" (Numbers 13:31-33).

> *Caleb had seen the exact same challenges as the other ten spies, but he came back believing God's promises, not seeing walls.*

*Everyone is giant-size? Really?* By forgetting God's promise that the land was theirs, the Israelites failed to believe, and the wall before them kept growing higher. In the first report they testified that there were *some* giants. But by the second report, *all* the people were huge. And their Wall of Fear and Doubt continued growing ever higher: "Next to them we felt like grasshoppers, and that's what they thought, too!" (Numbers 13:33).

*Like grasshoppers.* That's looking at men who were life-size (even if they were big) and seeing instead a horde of nineteen-foot bronze Thomas Jefferson statues they would have to conquer. When I looked up the anatomy of a grasshopper, the most common Middle Eastern species grows to about two inches long. And by anybody's standards, that is a tiny way to see yourself in the midst of tough challenges. It's no wonder the Israelites didn't have any confidence that the wall they were facing could ever come down. They had not only exaggerated the size of the enemy, they had completely minimized their own capabilities with God as their Conquerer. Now *that* is a serious attitude problem.

That is what mind-sets of fear, doubt, and unbelief do to walls. The walls lead us back into the wilderness, where life is never what it was meant to be. The walls don't get smaller; they continue to grow until we feel like a grasshopper next to a nineteen-foot statue. The walls teach us to fake fulfillment, pretending that life outside of the Promised Land is all we ever hoped for in the first place. The walls eventually distract us from what could have been . . . until the opportunity expires.

That is, unless we follow the lead of Joshua and Caleb, choosing to look beyond the walls to God's plan for our lives and living the victorious life that comes after a Faith Breakthrough.

Years later, when the Israelites finally entered the Promised Land, the first city they conquered was Jericho. As Joshua led them to victory, do you remember how God won? That's right: by tearing down the walls.

I have yet to meet someone who didn't struggle with these

unseen walls. But I have met many who failed to admit which wall they were facing. . . .

## DISCUSSION QUESTIONS

1. There is a difference between being content and being complacent. How can you tell the difference between having a satisfaction with what God has given you and settling for an unhealthy satisfaction with something less than God wants for you?

2. Ryan explains how walls can leave us restless. When you look around at our culture, which seems to be without rest, what do you see as the heart of the problem? What do you think the solution is?

3. Look back on your own upbringing. Can you think of times when your parents or other authority figures seemed to fake a sense of spiritual satisfaction when their actions spoke differently? How did this impact you?

4. What situations that seem overwhelming today are most likely to seem less of a big deal twenty years from now? How might you learn to see them from a healthier perspective?

# chapter five

# NAMING YOUR WALL

By now, I'm hoping you have already made up your mind that a life *without* Faith Breakthroughs is a terrible waste of God's blessings. It is a life behind walls of our own making, walls that hinder us from the very best that God has in store for us. These walls are stacked with the bricks of mistrust, low expectations, despair, and doubt. But it is not enough to talk about the general idea of the unhealthy mind-sets that hinder us. The walls in our lives need to be named so we don't forget they are there and so we remain focused on addressing the heart of the problem.

Recognizing your wall puts you on the path toward your breakthrough. On the other hand, I have never known anyone to experience a Faith Breakthrough without first acknowledging the wall.

Remember the wall in Berlin? In all, there were about 45,000 different sections of that infamous structure. I'm sure we humans have created *at least* that many walls from the unhealthy attitudes in our own lives.

For example, I've encountered people who are trapped behind Walls of Doubt. There is a Wall of Bitterness that has ruined countless relationships, and a Wall of Preoccupation with Past Hurts or Dysfunction that can seem to move in front of every positive step we try to make in our relationships. There are Walls of Pride and Anger that seem to never go away. And Walls of Unforgiveness that seem so high as to be unscalable. I've witnessed Walls of Unfeeling Ritual that rob people of fresh, genuine faith. I have seen Walls of Uncaring Rebellion that were built intentionally brick by brick. And I have never seen any of them come down by accident.

## DECLARING WAR ON THE WALL

By the time President Ronald Reagan arrived in Berlin in 1987, the infamous Wall had already been standing for over a quarter century. Of all the thousands of speeches that have been given in modern history, very few have been as history-changing as the one given that year near the Berlin Wall.

That is quite a statement, considering all of the great speeches that have been made through the years:

- Abraham Lincoln's famous words of comfort near the Gettysburg battlefield on November 19, 1863: *"Four score and seven years ago . . ."*

- Franklin D. Roosevelt's first inaugural address in 1933, and a borrowed line made famous: *"The only thing we have to fear is fear itself."*
- British Prime Minister Winston Churchill, during World War II, using his gravelly voice and indomitable spirit to rally his countrymen to keep on fighting, no matter the odds: *"I have nothing to offer but blood, toil, tears, and sweat."*
- Reverend Martin Luther King's resonating voice, on a steaming hot summer day in our nation's capital, fanning the flames of the Civil Rights Movement: *"I have a dream!"*

A historian might see that as the Speech Hall of Fame, but it would most certainly be incomplete. Among the most powerful words ever spoken pertained to the infamous Berlin Wall, in a simple speech given on April 21, 1987 . . . over dinner . . . to a dozen people . . . by Ingeborg Elz.

You recall the words spoken by this German housewife, right? The unforgettable words "get rid of this wall."

If you're not quite sure how Ingeborg Elz got into a short list of the world's most memorable speech-givers—and if her words sound eerily similar to those spoken by someone slightly more famous in front of the Berlin Wall that same year—there's a reason to hear the rest of the story. You don't have to be famous to utter powerful words about walls.

As you probably know, all presidents hire speechwriters to help them craft their most important speeches. In April 1987, Peter Robinson, President Reagan's favorite speechwriter, had been sent ahead of the president to West Berlin to prepare for a speech Reagan was to give at the Brandenburg Gate on June 12.

The speech was to take place on the 750th anniversary of the city of Berlin. Robinson traveled to Germany with an advance team of logistical experts and Secret Service agents two months ahead of time as part of the usual detachment of people sent ahead of a president's arrival in a foreign city.

In his outstanding book, *How Ronald Reagan Changed My Life*, Robinson offered insight into the writing of the Berlin Wall speech. He shared how he was at a dinner party with a group of about a dozen Berliners. His hosts were Dieter and Ingeborg Elz, he a banker and she a stay-at-home mother.[4]

To help Robinson better understand the mood of Berliners as he drafted his speech, some friends of his had asked their friends, the Elzes, if they would be kind enough to host a dinner for him. They were asked to gather together people from several different walks of life who lived in Berlin and then follow dinner with a time of discussion about their city. The dinner included businessmen, academics, students, and homemakers.

After dinner, Robinson launched the discussion time by sharing that earlier in the day he had spoken with a high-ranking American diplomat who lived in Berlin. When Robinson asked this diplomat about what Berliners thought about the Wall, he was told, "Oh, the people of Berlin have made a kind of *accommodation* with the wall over the years." After sharing this comment with the dinner guests, Robinson asked, "Is it true? Have you gotten used to it?"

Robinson recounts the long silence and then how one man sitting near him raised an arm and pointed. "My sister lives twenty miles in that direction," he said. "I haven't seen her in more than two decades. Do you think I can get used to that?" Others shared similar opinions, none remotely close to the view of the American diplomat.

That's when their petite hostess turned beet red with anger, made a fist with her hand, and pounded it into her other palm. "If this man Gorbachev is serious with his talk of *glasnost* and *perestroika*," she said, "he can prove it. He can get rid of this wall!"

As we look back through history from a modern perspective, that statement may seem obvious, but it wasn't necessarily the case when those words were spoken. Somebody had to stand up and point out the heart of the problem: it wasn't political confusion or lack of communication. In fact, the wall that was really holding them back was the physical wall that stood in Berlin. And Ingeborg Elz was the one who changed history by speaking that truth with conviction.

She spoke with such force, such spontaneity, and such heartfelt passion that her words made the rest of the discussion seem trivial in comparison. And it was at that dramatic moment that the speechwriter Robinson drew together the message he knew President Reagan needed to say. Robinson changed her words slightly, and the speech became, "Mr. Gorbachev, tear down this wall!"

However, even then, those words were almost never spoken.

Robinson wrote and submitted his speech to President Reagan. He made sure to tell the president that people in both West and East Germany would be listening to his words. And he recalls Reagan cocking his head as they talked and saying, "I really like the part about tearing down the wall." But then the speech was circulated among officials in the state department and National Security Council.

Some of the printable feedback received regarding the powerful phrase was that it was "naïve," would "raise false hopes," and was "needlessly provocative." As a result, people with a much higher pay grade than a speechwriter submitted their own draft to the president, minus the troublesome words "tear down this wall."

Robinson recalls seven different versions of the speech being drafted and discussed before the final one was approved and handed to Reagan at the Berlin airport. Not one of those revisions, including the last one Reagan was handed in the limousine on the way to the Berlin Wall, had the famous words in them. Yet, on the way to the site, President Reagan decided that the majority would not sway him. Like it or not, he was putting back in Robinson's suggestion—and Ingeborg Elz's slightly modified words.

In front of thousands of people at the Wall, and by radio and television to millions on the East German side of the Wall listening to him, he said, "Mr. Gorbachev, tear down this wall!"

And of course, the rest is history.

President Reagan's speech may not have been the catalyst that brought down the Wall. Many historians contend that there were far more important forces at work in the Eastern Bloc that were already causing the politics of the

Iron Curtain to erode. However, Reagan's speech dared to do something that no one with his power and authority had yet been willing to do: address the problem head-on. To name the heart of the problem. That is always the first step in seeing a wall come down.

## START BY PUTTING A NAME TO YOUR WALL

It's time to honestly write down what is holding you back from God's best today, to put a name to your wall.

Why a name? Two reasons. First, putting a name to your wall paints a target on it. By giving it a name (a Wall of Anger, or Fear, or Doubt, or Shame, or Pride) you can begin to draw on specific Scriptures and promises that speak to your specific situation, helping you find promises that can begin battering down your wall.

*Naming the heart of the problem is always the first step in seeing a wall come down.*

And second, putting a name to your wall proclaims clearly that you are ready for a Faith Breakthrough—which is why I'm going to ask you to name yours now on the next page.

When I was trying to identify my own wall, I asked three honest questions:

- Is there something in my life—a response to circumstances, an attitude about life, or a decision I've made—that is contrary to what God would want for me?
- When I spend time in prayer with the Lord, is there

a specific element of my life, heart, or feelings that keeps coming to mind?

- Are there poor decisions I have made in recent days that were rooted in an unhealthy mind-set?

When I asked those questions, the answer was clear. The wall that has held me back most often is the Wall of Fear, especially in light of our struggles with Lily. It's sometimes overwhelming to me that I can't keep her from any of the hard times that may be lurking around the corner. Lily's struggles are not my wall, but the fear that I feel has the danger to completely hold me back in my faith.

So I've given my wall a name and put a date below it. I'd like to invite you to do the same right now:

The wall that holds me back is the Wall of

_____

_____

DATE

Or, right after you pray about it, ask the Spirit of God to help you recognize your unseen wall. And if, after thinking and praying, you still can't come up with a single wall you're facing, then a wise thing to do is talk to your spouse, a close sibling, or a best friend. Ask them, "Do you see any unhealthy mind-sets in my life that you think are holding me back from God's best?" That kind of question, asked in humility, can be a tremendous help in isolating and naming your wall.

I need to be honest with you. This exercise was very hard for me, and it may be for you as well. I have spent all of my adult life sharing God's promises with others, but it was only when I was willing to confess the areas where my mind-set was holding me back that I really understood how precious those promises can be. Medicine doesn't do any good until there is a diagnosis and it is applied.

In my case, when it was (and is) my daughter's life and future at stake, I had to make an extremely difficult admission: "Lord, I am scared to death. I'm terrified that things aren't going to work out for her. And worst of all, I fear whether you will do anything to reverse what I dread in the future."

Those admissions may sound brutal, or even heretical, to you. But without naming my wall, the rest of this journey would have been a big charade. I cannot overstate the importance of being completely transparent before God as you personalize the wall. The rest of the book and the rest of your life depend on it.

**I cannot overstate the importance of being completely transparent before God as you personalize the wall.**

As a part of naming your wall, I'd also like to invite you to start mapping your breakthrough with your own personal account at www.FaithBreakthroughs.com. When you open an account, you're given your own section of the virtual wall we've built that you can see when you visit. You can choose to have the words you write be private. You can also choose to let other people in the Faith

Breakthrough community see your wall and breakthrough thoughts as a way to encourage them as they trust God for a Faith Breakthrough.

Whether you go online or not, it's time to admit to yourself something God already knows: the name of the wall that's been holding you back.

First Corinthians 14:8 says, "If the bugler doesn't sound a clear call, how will the soldiers know they are being called to battle?"

Putting a name to your wall is like sounding the battle cry, "This wall must come down!"

Now that you know your enemy, it's time to arm yourself for a Faith Breakthrough. And of all things, it begins with the power of a most unlikely weapon. . . .

## DISCUSSION QUESTIONS

1. Given what you've learned about walls, what would you say are some of the most common walls that people experience today?

2. Ryan pointed out several subtle dangers that walls create. Which one resonates most with you and why?

3. Ingeborg Elz confronted the lie on which Robinson was basing his entire speech. Who is the "Ingeborg Elz" God has put into your life to challenge you to confront falsehoods to which you are clinging?

4. Review the three questions you can use to identify your own walls (see pages 65–66). What did you learn as a result of answering these questions?

5. While our walls are not our circumstances, some of our most difficult walls can come as a result of circumstances in our lives. What situations in your life have led to your walls?

6. Are there walls (or at least areas of difficulty) in your life that you have a tendency to avoid naming or defining out of hurt or fear? Why do you think people have a tendency to do that?

# 2

# THE
# BREAKTHROUGH'S
# SECRET WEAPON

# chapter six

# THE POWER OF A PROMISE

Congratulations! The wall may be invisible, but you know it's there, because you have been bold enough to name it. It can never hold you back again without your knowing it. Your wall is marked for destruction.

Putting a name to your wall is a huge step, and you are now in position to get started on the best part of the process—tearing down your wall on the way to a Faith Breakthrough. It's time to recognize two important warnings, though.

## WARNING 1

You're about to uncover some powerful ways of moving past your wall, and there is a sequence to the steps involved. However, you'll also notice that not all dots are connected. This is not an accident. Like a gardener cultivating the growth of a beautiful plant, there are really no shortcuts: you will be responding to God's work in you far more than "making the breakthrough happen." There is a critical role for the Holy Spirit to play. Don't get ahead of him! As you read through these pages, take time once in a while to ask God these questions:

- Is there a place in my life where I am unwilling to trust that you want what is best for me?
- Are there areas of my heart that are failing to embrace the promise?
- Am I focusing on a surface issue and ignoring a deeper area of my life that needs to be addressed?

If you read through these chapters and follow the guidelines, you will probably be better able to cope with the walls in your life. But if you allow the Holy Spirit to guide you on this journey—even if that means that your course takes a few different turns than you find here—you will have experienced something far beyond what any of us can accomplish apart from him.

## WARNING 2

If you try to attack your wall with the wrong weapon, you're going to be disappointed. Not just any old weapon will do. I've seen the frustration people go through when they identify the walls in their lives and attack them with positive thinking, willpower, or even blame. The only weapon that will work is the one God has provided us.

The Bible gives us a clue with an amazing inside look at the life of Abraham, whose name actually means "father of many." Ironically, Abraham had no children until a very old age. Imagine the Wall of Frustration that could go up if you'd been promised a massive lineage only to have no children.

But he never lost hope in the promises God had given him, and he eventually was just that—the ultimate ancestor. Romans 4:20-21 tells us the secret of his legacy: "Abraham never wavered in believing God's promise. In fact, his faith grew stronger, and in this he brought glory to God. He was fully convinced that God is able to do whatever he promises."

Abraham broke through his wall in the only way that truly works: using the power of God's promises. And the God of Abraham has promises awaiting you, too—promises that have the power to carry you right past the wall in front of you.

You've probably been aware of the power of words all of your life, but not all words are created equal.

The Berlin Wall didn't fall because Ingeborg Elz proclaimed her desire that it would. But the Wall fell in part because Ronald Reagan *promised* it would fall. When words of *promise* are spoken by someone who has the power to back up those words, there is the potential for monumental change!

After Reagan echoed the historic words of Ingeborg Elz, he said something much less famous but just as impactful. He spoke of a promise:

> As I looked out a moment ago from the Reichstag,
> that embodiment of German unity, I noticed words

crudely spray-painted upon the wall, perhaps by a young Berliner, "This wall will fall. Beliefs become reality." Yes, across Europe, this wall will fall. For it cannot withstand faith; it cannot withstand truth. The wall cannot withstand freedom.[5]

Some young Berliner boldly made a statement, and the leader of the free world turned it into a promise: "This wall will fall."

How much more, then, should we have confidence when the Leader of the whole world, Jesus Christ, makes a promise? The promises of God are the secret weapon that can tear down every wall.

Are you convinced yet? Do you really believe that walls can come down through the power of promises? Perhaps you are thinking right now, *I've heard this before, and it doesn't work. I have read God's promises, and I've prayed, and I didn't get what I wanted!*

We need to understand that God's promises are powerful weapons, but they have to be used correctly.

## BEWARE OF THE MISUSE OF POWER

Why is it that young boys so often come up with great ideas at the very time their parents aren't home, especially the kind of great ideas that can easily lead to a catastrophe? At least that's the way it seemed for me when I was a boy.

I remember that when I was around ten years old, I was given a set of walkie-talkies. They were all the rage at the time, and mine were top-of-the-line, meaning they were black and heavy and they had a range of twenty or even thirty feet, so my friend and I could communicate at long distance—as long as we were actually close enough to hear each other anyway!

Those walkie-talkies were perfect for playing army and coordinating attacks. They wouldn't hold the attention of a modern-day boy for thirty seconds, but to us they were cutting-edge. One day when I was playing around with my walkie-talkies, my parents left me alone for a short while to run an errand. And that's when I came up with an idea I was convinced would change communication as we knew it.

It came to me after my parents had pulled out of the driveway: If using the nine-volt battery that powered my new walkie-talkies could allow me to talk to someone twenty feet away, *what would happen if the walkie-talkie had more power?*

It was like when the apple hit Newton over the head and he suddenly realized he'd discovered gravity. Or actually, it was probably more like when Emmett Brown, "Doc" in the movie *Back to the Future*, falls while he's hanging a picture in his bathroom, hits his head, and comes up with the idea for the flux capacitor. My idea, unfortunately, didn't work as well as either of theirs. Regardless, I was sure at the time that I'd stumbled upon a communications breakthrough all my own.

All I needed was more power for my radio, and the sky would be the limit in terms of how far away I could communicate with someone. Quick thinking took me to an old lamp that was ready for the trash heap anyway, and I was able to cut off the cord easily with a set of wire cutters. My great idea was that if I could just connect my walkie-talkie to the electric outlet instead of to that puny nine-volt battery, I could create a supercolossal galactic radio transponder. Forget twenty feet! I was about to create something so supercharged it would allow me to talk to people on the other side of the planet.

I went to work cutting off the plastic caps that went over the nine-volt battery in my walkie-talkie. Next, I twisted those small wires onto the larger open wires from the old lamp cord.

Now all I had to do was plug in my invention. I was all set to be the next Edison.

Unfortunately, the only thing I did share in common with Edison that day was that I learned something about electricity.

It's *fast*.

> My problem wasn't power—it was that I was ill equipped to access the tremendous power available, so I went about it the wrong way.

If you're a ten-year-old boy who is unwittingly trying to burn down the garage, electricity is fast enough to travel almost *instantly* from the wall to what had previously been known as my walkie-talkie, which I dropped like a burning snake, and that literally was melting in front of my eyes!

My problem wasn't in figuring out how to increase the power to my radio. I did that just fine, thank you. My problem wasn't power—it was that I was ill equipped to access the tremendous power available, so I went about it the wrong way.

There is a life-giving, life-sustaining, wall-breaking power in God's Word and, in particular, in God's promises. A power that spiritual walls simply cannot withstand. But many people miss out on that power because they don't understand how to tap into it. The result is frustration and disappointment, like running 220 volts into a nine-volt walkie-talkie.

Occasionally I talk to a church member who says, "Pastor, I want a breakthrough so badly, but it's just not working." Because our people have been taught over and over about the secret weapon of God's promises, I will always ask, "What promises are you claiming from God's Word?" And for those who can't get past their walls, they will invariably stumble. If it's a financial breakthrough they need, sometimes they will say, "I'm trusting God for the promise of being debt free!"

And I'll ask, "Where is *that* promise?" What I mean is that the Scripture speaks on the subject of debt, but it doesn't *promise* that God will wipe out your financial obligations. That misbelief short-circuits the promises of God. What God *does* promise is that he will provide for his children when they trust him and when they learn to live with a mind-set of contentment. God teaches that he rewards the diligent and that our hearts will focus where our treasure is placed. And while those promises may not take all the debt away (remember, your walls are not your circumstances!), they will radically impact the Wall of Greed or Lack of Discipline or Fear that is causing the debt to mount. Invariably, the debt will be addressed when the real promises are claimed.

When people discover the proper use of God's promises and begin to count on those promises, I have never seen those walls left standing over the course of time. Walls lose when they go up against God's promises!

God's Word is full of life and truth and power—and promises. That's exactly what you'll see in the stories of some of the "wall breakers" I know. You'll find their stories near the end of each chapter in this section. Each wall breaker is a member of our church, Bannockburn Baptist Church in Austin, Texas. They have all been a part of our journey through Faith Breakthroughs, and they have all claimed a promise of God and begun to turn that power loose on their unhealthy mindsets. Amazingly (and often miraculously) their walls started coming down. Real walls. Spiritual walls that, for many of them, had been standing for years before they came down.

> **Walls lose when they go up against God's promises!**

There is little doubt that President Reagan's promise, "This wall will fall," was a huge factor in the Berlin Wall's coming down just a couple of years later. And there is absolutely no doubt that God's Word, and God's promises, can power through the most difficult wall in front of you.

## GOD'S WORD AND THE VERY WORST OF WALLS

"But Pastor Ryan," I've been told by people in my church and elsewhere, "you don't understand; I was abused . . ." or, "I was betrayed . . ." or, "I was abandoned . . ." As I cross the country talking to people about making Faith Breakthroughs in their lives, it seems I always meet someone who feels that his or her story—his or her wall—is just too high for any words, whether those words are God's promises or otherwise.

I'm the first to admit how grateful I am for the home I grew up in, filled with so much love and light. I also know how blessed I've been to have a beautiful, godly wife and wonderful children who know and love the Lord. In comparison to lots of people I've met, I know I have suffered so little. But I also know that God's promises are true and that God's Word speaks of his Son, Jesus, who endured the suffering of the cross and whose words and light can break through the darkest of places. Even the darkness of a POW camp.

It was Christmas Eve 1967, and Lieutenant John McCain was being given another "mind-set adjustment session" by his sadistic Vietnamese captors. Shot down over Hanoi, McCain had joined a number of other American prisoners of war in the infamous prison they called the "Hanoi Hilton." On that day, McCain had been caught talking with another prisoner and was being beaten for his offense.

McCain later told of how one interrogator in particular delighted in brutality. He would approach McCain each day and demand that he bow before him. If McCain refused, he'd be struck in the face. But if he did bow, he'd be struck in the face anyway. So either way, this guard would smash his fist into the side of McCain's head every day, knocking him to the ground. In McCain's words, "These encounters were not episodic. They occurred every morning for nearly two years."

Try to imagine being trapped in that kind of setting every day for years. A place where high walls topped with barbed wire surround you and where daily doses of cruelty and torture await you . . . even on the day before Christmas.

That Christmas Eve, things got much worse than just a blow to the head. Late in the afternoon McCain was brought from his cell to the main interrogation room. He was tied to a chair and literally beaten unconscious.

The officers were the interrogators, and in McCain's words, they were the most brutal to the prisoners. The camp was also run by soldiers whom the Americans called gun guards. They wandered around the camp, carrying rifles on their shoulders. Many of these men had been so severely wounded in battle that it kept them from being shipped to the front lines. And it was these young men who supervised the prisoners' daily routines. They would let the men out of their cells to eat their meals or to bathe, and they were the ones who locked them back up in their cells when they were finished.

And so it was that, on a memorable night, Lieutenant McCain woke up from his beating around midnight. The regular night shift time for gun guards was from 10:00 p.m. to 4:00 a.m. As he came to his senses, McCain realized he was still tied to his chair and was in terrible pain.

That's when a gun guard entered the room.

McCain had never talked to this man, nor did he even remember making eye contact with him, something that was forbidden for the prisoners to do with their captors.

The young soldier stood inside the interrogation room for a moment and then quickly walked over to McCain. Silently, without once looking directly at or smiling at his prisoner, he loosened the ropes that bound him and left him alone in the room. Incredible relief flowed over McCain as the blood flowed back into his arms and legs, and he was able to sit up and even stand to stretch. A few minutes before his shift ended, that same gun guard returned, sat him back down in the chair, and tightened his ropes.

McCain knew that, without question, if that young man had been caught aiding an American prisoner, the best he could hope for would be to be shot. More likely, he would have been tortured to death in front of the other gun guards as an example of what would happen to those who aided the enemy. But no one knew what had happened that early Christmas morning except this unknown gun guard and Lieutenant John McCain.

Morning came, and it was Christmas Day. An officer came in and ordered the new guard to untie McCain and take him back to his cell. He arrived in time for the Christmas gift the prisoners were given. They were allowed to stand outside their cells for five minutes to exercise or just to stand there and look at the trees and sky.

It was during these minutes that McCain noticed the same young gun guard who had risked his life to loosen McCain's ropes approach him. McCain writes:

> He walked up and stood silently next to me. Again, he didn't smile or look at me. He just stared at the ground in front of us. After a few moments had passed he rather nonchalantly used his sandaled foot to draw a cross in the dirt. We both stood wordlessly looking at the cross until, after a minute or two, he rubbed it out and walked away.

The reason that day was so significant is revealed in the title of McCain's book, *Faith of My Fathers*.[6] I can just imagine that in the midst of that moment, he was drawn back to a promise he had heard early in life: "I will never leave you nor forsake you" (Hebrews 13:5, NKJV; see also Deuteronomy 31:8; Joshua 1:5).

That event became a turning point in McCain's life. As terrible as conditions would be for the next five years, he would know that no walls were too high for God's love to penetrate. Without a word—with just a picture of the Cross and the thousands of words it represents—God showed him that any wall, even the ones surrounding the Hanoi Hilton, could one day come down. It was the power of God's promise that kept McCain alive and expectant of better days. And that same power is available for you today, ready to carry you through—and beyond—your own walls.

In the book of Ephesians, the apostle Paul talks about what life was like for each of us before the Cross, when we were cut off from God and stuck on the wrong side of the wall. He says, "In those days you were living apart from Christ. You were excluded from citizenship among the people of Israel, and you did not know the covenant promises God had made to them. You lived in this world without God and without hope" (Ephesians 2:12).

Notice that the people who were living apart from Jesus were being robbed of one very important aspect of his presence: the promises God had made to them. They were without knowledge of God's promises, and so they saw life without the luxury of God and hope—an outlook that was ripe for unhealthy mind-sets. And then he concludes the thought by sharing what happened when the promises were reintroduced: "For Christ himself has brought peace to us. He united Jews and Gentiles into one people when, in his own body on the cross, he broke down the wall of hostility that separated us" (Ephesians 2:14).

Jesus' blood, shed on the cross, broke down the wall that

divided a fallen people from a holy God. And that same wall-breaking power is available to the believer for the rest of his or her life! If you have stayed the course, even in the worst of circumstances, then you know what it means to experience blessings whether the situation changes or not.

What if John McCain had never made it out of Hanoi? Would the promise he was clinging to have been any less powerful? I say no, because the promise extends beyond this world to the eternity awaiting those who trust and know Jesus. To forsake God's promises because the blessing doesn't come in the shape or form you had hoped is only robbing yourself. It could be that the circumstances may be about to change for the better. And it could be that God wants to bless you in the midst of those circumstances in a way that you can't humanly see or understand. The challenges you face are not an indicator of a lack of faith. They are instead an opportunity to express that faith.

Are you ready, then, to learn how specifically to use the power God gives us through his cross, through his Word, and within his promises to tear down your walls?

I'm not sure what voices are telling you that your wall can't come down. Perhaps you hear failed promises that you've made in the past that mock your efforts to try yet again. Or you might hear words from a specific person in the past (even someone linked to your wall) saying things like, "You will never amount to anything . . ." or, "What a crutch you have with your religion . . ." or, "How can I think you can take care of me, when you can't even take care of yourself?" or, "I left you for a reason; you're worthless!" or, "You don't need to forgive him . . . you need to 'overcome' him!" or, "Don't you realize how badly you've sinned? Do you really think that God is going to let you off the hook for that?"

I'm sure Satan will have a whole team of editors ready either to supply negative words or to get you to cut out from your speech (or even your thinking) any words you might say that sound like, "Lord, it's time for my wall to fall!"

Whispered words can lull us to sleep when action is needed. Words like, "Oh, it's not *that* big of a deal, that 'wall' in front of you," or, "That wall has been standing in your life for so long; you should just 'accommodate' for it."

Or you'll hear other voices saying that the idea of a wall coming down is just false or naive hope, or that tearing it down will do nothing but stir up problems and be needlessly provocative. "Just leave well enough alone. What you're about to do is going to be too hard!" the voices will say.

But don't listen.

Listen instead to the promises that await you, the promises God has been offering you all along.

## DISCUSSION QUESTIONS

1. As you think about any walls you identified in chapter 5, can you recall any times you've gotten into trouble by running ahead of the Holy Spirit? Explain.

2. The Bible makes clear that the only way to get past our walls is to know God and claim his promises. What are some other "weapons" that people try to use to overcome their walls?

3. Sometimes the best way to understand what God has promised is to acknowledge what he has *not* promised. For example, God

never promised that I would be happy all the time. Can you fill in this blank with other common non-promises? God never promised me _____.

4. The world is full of people like John McCain, who have had amazing breakthroughs in the midst of unthinkable struggles. Who do you think of when you are reminded of such faith heroes?

# Mike & Marisha
## WHEN WALLS BECOME BREAKTHROUGHS

*If you ever meet* Mike and Marisha, they'll be quick to proudly show off pictures of their children. But when Mike was young, his own father walked away from him. I'll never forget the day he described to me how it felt when, as a young boy, his dad called him into the living room. He and his two brothers sat down and heard their father explain that he was leaving home. To make matters worse, all their dad told them that morning was, "Your mother doesn't love me anymore and has asked me to leave." Only years later would Mike learn that his dad had been involved in an affair.

In the days after that speech, Mike's world began to fall apart, and his family right along with it. They faced incredible economic hardships. His mother had difficulty coping with the hurt while also trying to comfort her children. His brothers dealt with the pain in their own ways—sometimes with feelings of anger, sometimes with hearts of despair. Of course, because their mom was the "safer target," she became the object of much of their vengeance. As is often the case, the children did not comprehend the details of what took place. They only knew that things were no longer the same.

Up to those moments, Mike's expectations had been built upon a few important foundational truths: love and marriage were forever; his parents would always be there for him; and the God who loved him would protect him from pain. But in a moment—in one meeting with Dad—all the truths on which he based his mind-sets about life blew up in front of him.

As the family dealt with the crisis, they began to splinter, leaving Mike to bounce around among extended family members. Mike tried so hard, but it seemed that soon a Wall of Fear that he would never have a normal family himself blocked him from any kind of real commitment.

Mike spent his teen years on the move from his mother to his father to his grandparents and back to Mom. At every stop, he also felt pressure as he tried to deal with an angry older brother's resentment and a confused younger brother's detachment.

As a young adult, however, some circumstances in Mike's life shaped a dramatic transformation. He met Marisha when he was staying with his mother and her new husband. And as they fell in love, Marisha provided the motivation Mike needed to seek a better way. God's grace and power demonstrated to them both that that better way was more than a dream.

They began to claim—and live—God's promises for their lives. One promise they clung to was John 1:12-13: "To all who believed him and accepted him, he gave the right to become children of God. They are reborn—not with a physical birth resulting from human passion or plan, but a birth that comes from God." Several years into their marriage God brought Mike and Marisha to Austin, Texas, and to Bannockburn, the church where I am pastor. While attending a parents class I was teaching, they heard me talk about the importance of understanding the heritage we have received, good or bad, and choosing to hand it to the Lord. Mike came to see me at the church a few days after our first meeting. With tears in his eyes, he shared his heartache and disappointments from growing up in a dysfunctional family, but he also shared something with all of the determination a man can have. Mike was absolutely committed to provide a better way for his children, a life without the hindrances of the walls that destroy the home.

A few weeks later, during our dedication service on Sunday morning, I had the privilege of handing Mike and Marisha a copy of a Legacy Covenant they had crafted for themselves, a proclamation before God that they were choosing to walk in his promises for their family. In the years that have followed that special morning, I have had the privilege of watching the walls continue to fall in their lives. Mike is living beyond the hurt that comes from many of his childhood memories and instead is able to serve as a conduit of God's grace to his entire family. We were e-mailing back and forth recently about his journey to a breakthrough, and Mike reminded me of something powerful about the process of tearing down walls: "I'm glad to know that as my wall came down, Christ was not on the other side. He was right here with me, taking it apart."

Mike and Marisha know firsthand how powerful a Faith

Breakthrough can be in dealing with past hurts and pointing someone toward a special future. In the next chapter, you'll learn how you can discover a promise to break down the wall in your own life by drawing closer to the same God who transformed Mike and Marisha's family forever.

(chapter seven)

# A PROMISE DISCOVERED

There's a tremendous difference between having knowledge of a promise and taking ownership of that promise. And the difference between the two comes when the power of that promise is discovered for the first time—the moment when the promise becomes personal.

A letter written by William Stukeley recounts a spring afternoon in 1726 when his best friend—perhaps the most famous scientist of all time—shared a story with him over tea "under the shade of some apple trees." Stukeley wrote, "He told me, he was just in the same situation, as when formerly, the notion of gravitation came into his mind. It was occasion'd by the fall of an apple, as he sat in contemplative mood. Why should that apple always descend perpendicularly to the ground, thought he to himself. . . . Why should it not go sideways, or upwards? But constantly to the earth's center? Assuredly, the reason is, that the earth draws it. There must be a drawing power in matter."[7]

And so Isaac Newton recounted to his friend one of the most celebrated scientific discoveries of all time—the theory of gravity—and how it had been discovered by an apple unexpectedly falling from a tree near him.

Certainly Newton was not the first person to observe the falling fruit, nor was it the first time he had seen it. How, then, could it be called a discovery? While the apple had been seen before, and the falling had been seen before, the moment when the principles of what was really happening came alive to him changed his life—and an entire discipline of learning—forever.

The promises that will carry you to your breakthrough may be brand-new to you, or you may have heard them all your life. But a promise is not discovered until it is applied, until the lightbulb goes on and the promise gets personal: "That's not just a word to someone in the first century. That's a promise for me!"

## DISCOVERING THE THEORY OF "DISPERSION"

I grew up around airplanes. My father was a pilot, and a two-decade career in the Air Force gave way to many interesting ventures, including running the airport in our town. I spent many days doing odd jobs around that place, and as you might imagine, there's nothing that brings back memories for me like the smell of jet fuel in the morning!

I can't say I loved every minute of gassing and washing small planes, but the job had its perks: I got to enjoy a lot of father-son flights as I was growing up. Most of them were fantastic memories, but there is one exception I'll never forget.

Dad got a call at the office from one of our neighbors, sharing that her husband had passed away, and she had a very unique request. This old Texas rancher had always wanted to be cremated and to have his ashes scattered across his homestead.

She was calling to ask a simple favor: would we be willing to fly over their land and honor the last wishes of this beloved man by scattering his remains from the air?

Of course, as the boss's son, I was the obvious candidate for the job of sidekick on this unusual mission.

The day came, and the funeral director delivered a large plastic bag containing the man's ashes to us. Carefully, I carried the package to the Cessna 172 that was already warming up on the runway. The plane was a four-seat, single-engine aircraft that could fly relatively slow and seemed perfect for the task at hand.

Dad knew just where we were to go, and I knew it would be a short flight. We lifted off and quickly reached our cruising altitude of about 1,500 feet. We hadn't really coordinated how we were going to do this before lifting off, but how hard could it be? Dad assumed that we would talk about it when we got up in the air. I assumed, because he was busy flying the plane, that it was my responsibility to figure out what to do in order to scatter the ashes.

And here's where my very poor choice came in.

I wanted to be ready when we got to the spot, so I opened

up the bag containing the ashes as it sat in my lap. My father was busy flying, paying special attention to the angle of approach so we could make a dramatic entrance over the tree-lined hill where the bereaved family had gathered to watch. The cruising speed of a Cessna 172 is roughly 122 knots, or 143 miles per hour.

As soon as Dad said we were over the spot, I opened the window in order to stick the bag outside and distribute my powdery payload. That's when two things combined inside the plane that brought a discovery I wish I had never made.

With an incredible *whoosh!* the rush of air poured into the plane. It hit the open bag of ashes with a wall of wind, and Dad and I experienced a small hurricane of dust, ashen clouds of darkness that enveloped the cockpit in a matter of moments.

Let's put it this way. It's cute to see a dog with its head out the window in a car going 40 miles an hour. There is nothing cute about a deceased man's remains suddenly being sucked out of a baggie by wind traveling at 143 mph! I'm sure a small amount of his ashes did get spread somewhere over south Texas, but most of the ashes were worn by my father and me.

If we had needed to make an instrument landing right then, we would have been in serious trouble! Everything—and I mean literally every square inch inside the plane, from the inside of all the windows to every single instrument—was covered in a thin layer of ash. It took a few days to get all of the remnants out of our clothes and hair, but the picture will be in my mind forever.

Unfortunately, in life some things are discovered the hard way. But God's promises, which are just as true as the laws of science, are just waiting for someone who is ready to pay attention. For those who do, a host of blessings await.

## WHY GOD ENCOURAGES US TO SEEK OUT HIS PROMISES

Just before Jesus was arrested and went to trial, he was alone with his disciples, a handpicked group of beloved friends. These were men with whom he'd spent every day for the past three years. These were men he would die for, along with a world of others, in just a few hours.

In this upper room he began talking with his disciples about how they could continue to honor him even after he left them. He said, "Those who accept my commandments and obey them are the ones who love me. And because they love me, my Father will love them. And I will love them and reveal myself to each of them" (John 14:21).

Jesus promises to reveal himself. But that disclosure comes in the context of a committed relationship, which is very much the way we reveal ourselves. We reveal little of who we are to a stranger. We reveal a little more to someone who is a nodding acquaintance. Even more to a coworker, perhaps; more still to a friend. The more intimate the friend, the more we reveal about ourselves. And to that most intimate of friends, our spouse, we reveal the most.

Why?

Because the secret of who we are is a precious thing, perhaps the most precious thing we have to share. And we don't want to share that with just anyone. We want to share our deepest thoughts, goals, and dreams with someone we love and who loves us, someone to whom we can entrust our heart.

## DISCOVERY AND THE MARRIAGE RELATIONSHIP

In my relationship with my wife, Lana, she feels loved when I pursue her, when I take the time to listen to her, and when I seek to draw out what she is feeling in her deepest being. She doesn't reveal what is on her heart in a casual, matter-of-fact way. Why? Because she is not interested in the exchange of information; she is interested in the growth of the relationship.

When I get frustrated with that process, I will sometimes say to her, "Can we get to the point?" But when I do that, I reveal something about myself. I reveal that I am more interested in gathering information or getting on to "the next important thing I'm working on" than I am in growing the relationship.

My wife, like most wives with their husbands, wants to be pursued; she wants me to take a deep interest in her. In the Song of Solomon, God's handbook on courtship and marriage, Solomon's bride says to him, "Draw me after you and let us run together!" (Song of Solomon 1:4, NASB). Her husband's taking the lead in drawing her out—her thoughts, her dreams, her fears, her goals—brings an intimacy that draws them even closer together.

In other words, when I kick into discovery mode with my wife to sincerely know her more (even after nearly twenty years of marriage), I prove my love for her! And in turn, my pursuit motivates her to reveal more of her heart to me.

I have a psychologist friend who encourages husbands to ask their wives, "Is there more?" when they pause in a conversation.

And there always is!

And so it is with God. He, too, is interested in an ever-growing relationship with us. Revelation is the means he uses to draw us into a deeper relationship with him, primarily through his Word, the Bible. In our super-busy lives, we can trivialize the relationship when we get frustrated with him and demand that he "get to the point." Or we can magnify the relationship, and delight him, when we seek to discover more about him, when we say, "Lord, is there more?"

And the answer he gives us is always yes.

There is always more truth, more love, more understanding, more forgiveness, more grace, and more mercy. More of his Word we can learn and memorize and share.

He is *the God of more*!

If we are willing to search, if we will actively pursue all that God has to say to us in his Word and through prayer, we will find he progressively reveals more and more to us.

"No eye has seen, no ear has heard . . . what God has prepared for those who love him" (1 Corinthians 2:9)! And each revelation is designed to draw us deeper and deeper into the relationship. I prove my relationship with God just as I do with my wife—by engaging in a process of discovery whereby he can reveal his heart. It is our hearts that God pursues and his heart that he wants us to pursue, which is why he says, "You will seek Me and find Me, *when* you search for Me with all your heart" (Jeremiah 29:13, NKJV, emphasis added). Notice something else about that verse: it doesn't say, "You will seek blessing and find blessing," or, "You will seek a problem-free life and find a problem-free life."

It says, "You will seek *Me* and find *Me*." Never forget that the end goal of a breakthrough is not things, or a mind-set, or a better situation. The ultimate objective is to know God himself, to experience the intimacy with him that is the ultimate fulfillment. The promises we will discover are the overflow of who God is and who he is shaping us to become.

## ARE YOU READY TO DISCOVER HIS PROMISES?

It is in the process of discovery that your mind-sets begin to change. You begin to mine the treasures of hope, help, courage, life, and love that you will need to power through your walls—to make that Faith Breakthrough. And while there are thousands of promises from God in the Old and New Testaments, it is important to discover them in a personal way. Until you take ownership of the promises, they are simply words on a page written for somebody else.

*The promises we will discover are the overflow of who God is and who he is shaping us to become.*

This process, while profound, is also very practical. It is critical that you understand how to identify the promises without misrepresenting the words God has given. Far too many people have led lives of disappointment because they mishandled the Scriptures only to believe in a lie.

Contrary to popular opinion, it is not necessarily God's will that you live a pain-free life. Anyone who says otherwise is offering up fool's gold. Instead, you must focus on the clear, and better, commitments that God has made to you by following a simple process.

## WHAT DOES THE BIBLE SAY ABOUT MY WALL?

Start with the obvious: seek to discover what the Bible says specifically about the mind-set, or mind-sets, related to your wall. You can begin in the concordance of your Bible, or you might conduct an online search using one of the many useful Bible sites available. Helpful topical Bibles have been published for just such a task, as have multitudes of books that outline God's promises in unique situations.

Of course, you can also inquire of a trusted pastor or friend who has studied the Bible extensively.

Don't just look up passages that relate to your wall directly. Search also for verses that deal with the "positive opposite" of your wall. For example, if you are dealing with a Wall of Resentment, look for promises related to gratitude, thankfulness, and waiting on God.

Once you have identified the key passages, you are ready to draw out the promises. These promises usually come in three forms:

*There are promises he made to everyone.*
These are universal promises God has made to every person for all times. For example, Psalm 31:23-24 speaks to all people who will choose to be faithful:

> Love the LORD, all you godly ones! For the LORD
> protects those who are loyal to him, but he harshly
> punishes the arrogant. So be strong and courageous,
> all you who put your hope in the LORD!

Clearly, the Lord promises to preserve the faithful. We can take that to the bank!

***There are promises he made to others that demonstrate his character.***

God made some promises to individual people at unique times in history. It would be irresponsible to claim that these are also made to everyone, but we do have the freedom to draw conclusions about God. After all, the same one who made those promises is at work today!

The book of Job is an account of a man who faced inconceivable difficulties. In the midst of the struggle, Job clung to a profound conviction of what he had learned about his God: "But he knows where I am going. And when he tests me, I will come out as pure as gold" (Job 23:10).

That certainty was born out of a lifelong walk with God that transcended Job's situational pain, and it was eventually realized when God later spoke to him, restored him, and blessed him immeasurably. If you're facing the difficult Wall of Disappointment, this prayer would certainly be appropriate:

> *Lord, you promised Job that you would use his trials to bring out the best in him, and you did. I rejoice despite my circumstances, because you are a God who brings joy to your children in your own time.*

***There are promises that are implied by his commands.***

The Bible makes it clear that our heavenly Father wants good things for his children. With that assurance, we can be confident that anytime he demands something of us, it is because of the promise of something better. Like a loving mother who commands her child not to touch a hot stove, the rules we live by are meant to point us toward a better way, not to make us miserable. When God gives an order, a promise can't be far away.

Look for the promises behind every command. Philippians 2:14-15 gives us a clear command for living: "Do everything without complaining and arguing, so that no one can criticize you. Live clean, innocent lives as children of God, shining like bright lights in a world full of crooked and perverse people."

For anyone facing a Wall of Bitterness, there is both a negative warning and a positive alternative, leading to a confident prayer that moves us toward the breakthrough:

> *Lord, Paul instructed a persecuted church not to be resentful because they would shine like stars in the universe. I claim the promise that I can be in on your eternal plan by trusting you even when things don't go well.*

Regardless of the wall you are facing, there is a corresponding promise just waiting to be discovered. The search may take some time, but I can promise it will be worth the effort.

Still not convinced that you can discover the promises you need? I want to share a few promises with you. You'll find many more promises like these at www .FaithBreakthroughs.com as well as tips and links to help you do your own breakthrough research so you can discover and pursue God's heart on your own.

*Regardless of the wall you are facing, there is a corresponding promise just waiting to be discovered.*

As you look at these verses, here's my prayer for you:

> *Lord, thank you for revealing more of your heart, more of your love, more of your hope, more of your help—more of yourself to us. Help us seek out and discover the promise or promises you have for us, and teach us how to use your life-changing, powerful Word to tear down the walls we're facing.*

If your wall is regret, consider starting with the following promises:

- The Lord is a shelter for the oppressed, a refuge in times of trouble. (Psalm 9:9)
- Those who know your name trust in you, for you, O Lord, do not abandon those who search for you. (Psalm 9:10)
- But the Lord your God refused to listen to Balaam. He turned the intended curse into a blessing because the Lord your God loves you. (Deuteronomy 23:5)
- For God has said, "I will never fail you. I will never abandon you." (Hebrews 13:5)
- I will not abandon you as orphans—I will come to you. (John 14:18)

If your wall is disappointment:

- Now we see things imperfectly, like puzzling reflections in a mirror, but then we will see everything with perfect clarity. All that I know now is partial and incomplete, but then I will know everything completely, just as God now knows me completely. (1 Corinthians 13:12)

- I look up to the mountains; does my strength come from mountains? No, my strength comes from GOD, who made heaven, and earth, and mountains. He won't let you stumble, your Guardian God won't fall asleep. Not on your life! Israel's Guardian will never doze or sleep. GOD's your Guardian, right at your side to protect you—shielding you from sunstroke, sheltering you from moonstroke. GOD guards you from every evil, he guards your very life. He guards you when you leave and when you return, he guards you now, he guards you always. (Psalm 121:1-8, THE MESSAGE)

If your wall is ritual (overcoming legalism or perfectionism):

- Thank God for this gift too wonderful for words! (2 Corinthians 9:15)
- God saved you by his grace when you believed. And you can't take credit for this; it is a gift from God. (Ephesians 2:8)
- For the wages of sin is death, but the free gift of God is eternal life through Christ Jesus our Lord. (Romans 6:23)
- But the Lord said to her, "My dear Martha, you are worried and upset over all these details! There is only

one thing worth being concerned about. Mary has discovered it, and it will not be taken away from her." (Luke 10:41-42)

If your wall is fear and anxiety:

- Let us hold tightly without wavering to the hope we affirm, for God can be trusted to keep his promise. (Hebrews 10:23)
- For he will be like a tree planted by the water, that extends its roots by a stream and will not fear when the heat comes; but its leaves will be green, and it will not be anxious in a year of drought nor cease to yield fruit. (Jeremiah 17:8, NASB)
- Be anxious for nothing, but in everything by prayer and supplication with thanksgiving let your requests be made known to God. (Philippians 4:6, NASB)

If your wall is shame (feeling like you've fallen too far or done too much wrong to be forgiven or acceptable to God):

- If we confess our sins to him, he is faithful and just to forgive us our sins and to cleanse us from all wickedness. (1 John 1:9)
- Therefore, since we have so great a cloud of witnesses surrounding us, let us also lay aside every encumbrance and the sin which so easily entangles us, and let us run with endurance the race that is set before us, fixing our eyes on Jesus, the author and

perfecter of faith, who for the joy set before Him endured the cross, despising the shame, and has sat down at the right hand of the throne of God. (Hebrews 12:1-2, NASB)

If your wall is doubt (or confusion):

- But you must remain faithful to the things you have been taught. You know they are true, for you know you can trust those who taught you. You have been taught the holy Scriptures from childhood, and they have given you the wisdom to receive the salvation that comes by trusting in Christ Jesus. All Scripture is inspired by God and is useful to teach us what is true and to make us realize what is wrong in our lives. It corrects us when we are wrong and teaches us to do what is right. God uses it to prepare and equip his people to do every good work. (2 Timothy 3:14-17)

If your wall is bitterness (an unwillingness to forgive):

- Get rid of all bitterness, rage, anger, harsh words, and slander, as well as all types of evil behavior. Instead, be kind to each other, tenderhearted, forgiving one another, just as God through Christ has forgiven you. (Ephesians 4:31-32)

There are so many more verses, and walls, that could be named (and that you can find at www.FaithBreakthroughs .com). But tearing them down starts with discovery of

God's promises: discovering a passage or promise that you can hold on to and trust God for to make a Faith Breakthrough in the near days to come. A promise that can prove to be the turning point in your life and life story.

## A PROMISE DISCOVERED AND A WAR HERO

Alvin York was the most decorated soldier of World War I. He received the Medal of Honor and more than forty other decorations for his service during the war. But did you know that all the men whose lives he saved, and all the medals he won, can be traced back to a promise discovered?

Gary Cooper won the 1942 Academy Award for his portrayal of this war hero in the classic movie *Sergeant York*.

Alvin York grew up in one of the poorest parts of Tennessee. Family struggles led to a life of bare survival and sin. Perhaps his only redeeming accomplishment in his early life was becoming a crack shot with a rifle. All of that changed in 1914, when York became convinced that his life needed to change. He surrendered his life to Jesus Christ, and to the shock of all those who knew him, he quit drinking, gambling, and fighting, and he even got married.[8]

Not long after the United States declared war on Germany, York got his draft notice. Not convinced that a Christian should go to war, he attempted to seek conscientious objector status but was turned down. Before he knew it, Alvin York was in the infantry, where he quickly established himself as the best shot in his company. But he still had grave misgivings about going to war.

During a time of leave, York sought God for a resolution

to his dilemma. As he read the Gospel of Matthew, York came to the place where Jesus is asked whether he should pay taxes or not. And Jesus' answer? "Well, then . . . give to Caesar what belongs to Caesar, and give to God what belongs to God" (Matthew 22:21).

He read that verse over and over and realized that God had given him an answer. There were responsibilities due to one's government and those to one's God. He discovered a promise inside that command—the assurance that God would honor his yielding to authority and would guide his next steps.

This passage in Matthew became something York held on to with all his heart. The promise that God would honor his patriotism and service changed his whole mind-set toward serving. He was free to serve in the army and to give his life to the Lord. York took that promise and went back to his unit and told his commander of his decision to stay in the army. Soon he and his whole division shipped out for France and eventually to the front lines.

On October 8, 1918, Corporal Alvin C. York and sixteen other soldiers under the command of Sergeant Bernard Early were dispatched before sunrise to take command of a critical railroad station. Due to a misunderstanding of their map, these seventeen men mistakenly ended up behind enemy lines. A brief firefight ensued that resulted in great confusion, and a huge number of German troops, thinking they were surrounded, surrendered to the Americans.

Unfortunately, once the Germans realized the Americans were so few in number, they signaled to a group of machine gunners, still on the hill overlooking the scene, to turn their fire away from the front and toward their own troops. After ordering the German soldiers to lie down, the machine gunners opened fire, resulting in the deaths of nine Americans instantly, including York's best friend in the outfit.

With all of York's ranking officers wounded or dead, command was turned over to him. It was up to him now to silence the machine guns.

By the time he was done advancing alone, twenty-five Germans were dead on the hill above them. In all, York and his men silenced thirty-five machine guns and took 132 German officers and soldiers as prisoners.

With York in the lead, nine Americans herded over a hundred prisoners back to the American lines—and the rest is history. But far too few realize that history was shaped by a promise discovered—Matthew 22:21—that changed Alvin York's life forever.

## WHEN GOD'S WORD READS OUR OWN LIVES . . .

I'm amazed how many times in my own prayers, or when I'm studying to give a sermon or message, I start out reading God's Word and discover that God's Word is reading me. If we just dig in and start reading, very often God's Holy Spirit guides our search to that very verse or promise we need, just like he did with Alvin York who sought his counsel as a reluctant soldier in World War I . . . and just like he does in our lives today.

Promises don't mean a great deal to us until they become personal—until we recognize that the God of the promises is not talking to some nameless person who is far better qualified for the guarantees he offers, but he is talking to us.

Lily's first year of life was full of moments when crisis led me to the Scriptures. When those promises began to read more like a letter than a history book to me, my heart began to change. But I also discovered that those passages often seemed to speak to others who weren't going through the heartache and helplessness of caring for a child who was hurting. As a way to encourage others—and to tell about God's faithfulness in our own lives—I occasionally included updates on Lily's condition on my blog. This Web page included daily—and sometimes hourly—updates on her condition and how others could pray specifically. Over the course of the ordeal, we were comforted to know that over five thousand people were checking in regularly and praying for our little girl.

> *When those promises began to read more like a letter than a history book to me, my heart began to change.*

In the dark hours following Lily's heart surgery on January 25, 2007, I wrote the following thoughts that offer a glimpse into my own discovery and posted them to my blog:

> I sent Lana to the Ronald McDonald House room last night to get some much-needed rest and stood watch solo in Lily's room. She can't be picked up, and so my job is pretty much limited to comforting her and putting her pacifier back in her mouth.
>
> It is the first time I have really been able to exhale and spend some time on extended prayers of gratitude. I was reading back through some of my own notes, and it's always interesting to see what meant the most after the storm was

over. Psalm 20 has been really important to me this week. It's actually a prayer of David's warriors for their king's safety and victory, but the promises and prayers fit quite nicely with my own cries this week.

In verse one, the psalm says, "In times of trouble, may the LORD answer your cry. May the name of the God of Jacob keep you safe from all harm."

During the surgery, as I kept reading this passage, I found this particular description of God to be really intriguing. It is making it clear that God's protection was something to be sought after. But God was described here as the God of Jacob. Why Jacob? Well, the preacher in me would say it's because Jacob represents all of Israel, God's chosen nation, and all of his descendants. But the scared dad in me was reminded of Genesis 32, where Jacob wrestled with God as he boldly asked for a blessing. Did God answer? Yes, but not without trial. Jacob limped away with a blessing, and a very sore hip.

That's the irony of God I'll never understand, but can really appreciate after the storm. God's richest blessings come only through pain. To be honest, I'm just overconfident enough that trials are the rare times I tend to desperately cry out to God. The worst and most arrogant part of human nature is that we think we are actually doing it on our own when things are going okay.

While I was studying last night, Dr. Gertz, one of the pediatric cardiologists, came in and woke up a finally sleeping and completely peaceful baby with the words "I'm so sorry, Lily, but I'm going to have to agitate you now." And she proceeded to poke and prod and push to diagnose and treat and make a little progress. Of course, Lily began to scream and groan in her weak little drug-induced way that she has right now and kept looking at me as if to say, "Why don't you DO something???" She had tubes hanging everywhere at the time, and they had both of her IV-laden arms tied to the bedrails to keep her from pulling on the life-giving lines.

I wanted badly to be able to tell her that her dad was only allowing all the pain and discomfort so that she could get stronger, that one day she could leave this place and do greater things than before. I was actually protecting her by making her vulnerable. That's a father's job.

And then, at 3:00 a.m., I thanked God in a whole new way for our last four months. For the first time, I really thanked him even for allowing this to happen.

Lana just walked back in and said, "You can't preach on Sunday, so you're going to preach to them now, huh?" Maybe so. Forgive me. I just wanted to let the record show that we're not just thankful for God making her well. We're also thankful for God teaching us when she hasn't been well, and we're going to trust him whether the future holds good things or more challenges. He's good either way.

There have been over 5,000 visits to Lily's page. I can't help but imagine that there might be some who are reading these updates who have only seen God at work from afar—and who have never trusted him personally. The greatest blessing of my life is knowing Christ, and the greatest gift I could offer you is the promise that you can know him too.

Romans 10:9 gives us the promise: "If you confess with your mouth that Jesus is Lord and believe in your heart that God raised him from the dead, you will be saved."

God loves you very much—he doesn't just love the Rush family—and I pray that you can have that same fellowship today. That would be the greatest outcome of this whole trial.

Okay, now I'll stop rambling. God is good, but he's not just good because things went well. He's been good all along.

For the first time in the entire ordeal, I realized that the trials did not negate the promises, but verified them. I would never in a million years wish harm upon my daughter, but even in the midst of the pain, God was keeping his Word.

We've seen, then, that a Faith Breakthrough begins with a promise discovered. But our look at promises, and at a Faith Breakthrough, doesn't stop with just discovering something in God's Word that fits our circumstance and faces the wall before us, because it's not enough to just discover a promise. We must also choose it in order to break through.

## DISCUSSION QUESTIONS

1. When Jesus was talking to his disciples about trusting his promises, he mentioned the importance of knowing him first. How important is it to know Jesus personally before you can trust his promises? Is it possible to really trust someone you do not know? Why or why not?

2. Think back to the time in your life that you felt closest to God. What was happening that cultivated that intimacy? Why do you not experience that all the time? How does your level of personal time with God affect your day-to-day mind-set?

3. Brainstorm a game plan for discovering new promises related to the walls in your life. What are some ways you plan to explore what God has to say to you? Most important, how can you ensure you'll take quiet time with God so He can speak to you personally about His promises through the Scriptures?

4. When you read Ryan's thoughts in the midst of Lily's surgery and recovery, he talks about the promise God offers of forgiveness that is available to all who trust him. Have you counted on that most important of promises? Share your story with others of how you came to know of Jesus' love and sacrifice for you.

5. Have you found a promise in God's Word that you believe may lead to a Faith Breakthrough? If so, and if you feel comfortable, share your discovery with others.

# Mort & Anna

## WHEN WALLS BECOME BREAKTHROUGHS

*Today Mort and Anna* couldn't look any more happy or carefree. But a number of years ago, they stood behind towering Walls of Shame and Guilt that had sprung up from Anna's choosing to have an abortion. She had been told by so many that this would be a simple solution to a profound crisis, but it had actually made everything even more of a problem.

From the moment Anna walked out of the clinic that day, she was keenly aware of the loss she had just experienced, a loss that would haunt her for years to come. After Mort and Anna were married and began having children, Anna was consumed by thoughts of what could have been in the life of her unborn child. Every birthday was a reminder of another birthday that would never be celebrated. She longed to experience the grace and love of God, but she felt that her actions had pushed her out of qualification for such mercy.

"For many years I knew I wanted God, but I honestly didn't think he wanted me," she later confided.

Anna lived behind a Wall of Shame that threatened to ruin her life, her family, and her marriage. But one day Anna and her husband heard the Good News of Jesus. Someone explained that receiving forgiveness has nothing to do with what we have done or can do, but is based only on what God has done for us by sending his only Son to die for all of those sins. Mort and Anna received forgiveness that day and have never been the same. A precious promise changed their lives forever: "So now there is no condemnation for those who belong to Christ Jesus" (Romans 8:1).

After claiming this incredible promise and learning to walk in God's grace, all of a sudden the most hurtful parts of her past have become Anna's greatest opportunity for ministry. She volunteers her time leading small groups of women who are dealing with the sorrow of abortion—sharing with them the love and forgiveness available to them from a God who loves them dearly.

And as if moving past the Wall of Shame weren't enough, Mort and Anna have been blessed in another way: they are the proud parents of seven beautiful daughters!

Change began for Mort and Anna when they understood that not only is there incredible power in a promise, but "a promise discovered" provides both a way out and a path toward God's best.

Mort and Anna know what it means to overcome walls through the power of a Faith Breakthrough.

# chapter eight

# A PROMISE CHOSEN

Every one of us can think of times when we knew all we needed to know to get started on a project, but failed to actually get started because of distractions, confusion, or lack of interest. We face a similar danger with promises: just because we know what to do doesn't mean we've experienced a breakthrough.

The book of James talks about the difference between hearing the promises and living by them: "Don't just listen to God's word. You must do what it says. Otherwise, you are only fooling yourselves. For if you listen to the word and don't obey, it is like glancing at your face in a mirror. You see yourself, walk away, and forget what you look like" (James 1:22-24).

Far too many people have uncovered the treasure of a

promise only to walk away unchanged simply because they never took ownership of that promise.

I'm reminded of a sermon illustration I once used that seemed like a better concept than it was an actual action plan. That Sunday morning I found myself next to a firefighter, wondering what I had gotten myself into. That's because he was standing with me seventy feet up, almost touching the ceiling of our church auditorium as I was getting ready to step off a thin platform onto nothing but air!

*We face a similar danger with promises: just because we know what to do doesn't mean we've experienced a breakthrough.*

It seemed like a great idea in the safety of my study. Earlier in the week, I had been working hard on my sermon on the topic of the Wall of Fear. While sitting in my study, the idea came to me of rappelling, an obvious occasion when you have to trust in something (like your harness, the rope, your carabiner, the person on belay below you). And most of our congregation is aware of my fear of heights.

When it was only theory, rappelling seemed perfect. I called a friend of mine who works for the Austin Fire Department and is also a member of our church. I knew he was an expert at these things, so I shared with him my great idea for that Sunday's sermon.

How about if, on Sunday morning, he and I hid up in the rafters of our very tall church sanctuary? Then, when it was time for the sermon to start, instead of me just walking out onto the platform, I—the fearless pastor—would rappel straight down seventy feet, land safely on the stage, and begin my message? Unfortunately, the firefighter friend thought it was a great idea as well.

The answer to the question I'm sure some of you are asking is, yes, a video does exist of what happened that Sunday. You can see it at www.FaithBreakthroughs.com.

Let's go back to the moment when I was looking over that ledge at the people and sharp objects far below me. Up until the moment I got strapped in, I was just thinking what a great object lesson this would be for the congregation. But the one who had the greatest lesson coming was me.

If you've never rappelled, it's not the most natural thing to do. You stand up some place that is way too high. Then you stand way too close to the edge. And then your friend smiles at you and says, "Go!" and you actually step backward and prove the law of gravity.

Of course, it helped that my friend knew exactly what he was doing and was more than worthy of my trust. It also helped that he was up there with me, assuring me that the locking mechanism would stay locked and that I wouldn't end up as the top-rated video on YouTube.

*All the knowledge was just theory until I trusted my life to the promises I had received.*

But whether it was a controlled descent or not seemed irrelevant at the moment it was time to step away from the platform. All the knowledge was just theory until I trusted my life to the promises I had received. It was in that one big step backward that I really chose the promise of protection and safety. And without that step, I would have missed out on a great memory that I'll enjoy for the rest of my life.

## WHY WALL BREAKING IS CONFIRMED WITH A PROMISE CHOSEN

I've already shared how God's Word, and especially his promises, has the power to blast through spiritual walls. In the last chapter, I asked you to grab your Bible and start looking up promises that can attack your wall. But while discovering promises is the first step, the second one is a doozy.

Making a Faith Breakthrough involves something more foundational, more serious, and frankly more challenging than mere discovery. It challenges a person, often in the midst of a trial that has led to his or her wall, to trust that what God says in that promise is true. The choice to trust requires us to lean back into the risk of the lifeline, our only hope, until we land safely on the platform below— like I had to do in not one but *two* morning services (with the second try significantly less stressful than the first).

Let me say again that some things people think are promises are not. It is important to evaluate the lifeline you're about to choose before relying on its security. Remember, God does not promise that we won't have trials and tests, or that we'll bypass pain and suffering. He does promise a way through those things here on earth, and he does promise us a life without tears or sickness or sadness or death in the world to come!

In our days on earth, God doesn't promise that all our investments will triple or that we'll never go bankrupt or that we'll never get sick or die. But he does promise us life and hope, freedom from anxiety, courage, forgiveness, and a hundred other things we can claim in this life—as well as the promise of eternal life with him after death.

No one is asking you to lean back on an uncertain rope that was never intended to support your dreams. Texans love their football, but there is no promise that the Dallas Cowboys won't lose, because there is no biblical promise that says they'll always win (even though my brother-in-law wishes there were!). It's a fruitless endeavor to trust in false promises, and even more dangerous to make wrong choices based on them.

Rather, it's when we choose to trust—not just in the promises of God, but in the God of the promises—that amazing things can happen . . . even in the most challenging times and circumstances.

Here are four things we teach at Bannockburn to those in the early stages of learning a promise chosen:

1. **A promise chosen starts with prayer.** The first and most important part of choosing God's promises is to pray those promises to God. Let him know what you have found in his Word, and express to the Lord that you are choosing to walk in that promise. I cannot overstate the power and importance of this step! When we pray, things begin to change. And when we fail to pray, I can promise you that things will not be the same as they would have been had we prayed for them.

   At Bannockburn, one of our four core values is "prayer with expectation." Expectant prayer is more than wishing things will come true; it is boldly asking for what God is fully capable of doing and looking forward to his answer.

2.  **A promise chosen requires commitment.** Before taking
    one step forward, you must determine that there is no
    turning back. Always remember that actions dictate
    feelings, not the reverse. If you feel like you want to
    go back to life behind your wall because "it's just not
    working" or "the change isn't happening fast enough,"
    you cannot allow your feelings to dictate your action.
    Don't wait until you feel like trusting the promise you've
    claimed. Get moving in faith. Amazingly, when you
    start moving, the feelings change—but your feelings
    will change only after you start moving in line with
    your commitment.

3.  **A promise chosen requires self-control.** Do you
    know what the word *self-control* means in the Bible? It
    literally means "to pull in the reins." That's the picture
    of a horse running away and its rider reining it in to
    stop it. When challenges come, you will be tempted
    to think, *I'm going back to hating that person. Just look
    at what he did now.* If you let negative thoughts run
    wild and don't pull in the reins, your emotions can
    take you away from where you want to go, away from
    God's best.

4.  **A promise chosen requires having a plan.** Aristotle
    once stated, "You stand a far better chance of hitting
    the target if you can see it." Those words may sound
    obvious, but they carry a great deal of simple truth we
    often forget: having a plan provides an important nudge
    to get moving.

The difference between goals and dreams is that goals involve assigning a timetable in which you plan to arrive there. Clearly, some elements of a breakthrough cannot be placed on a calendar, but some elements of claiming God's promises allow—and even require—a plan. For example, you can determine right now to memorize three key promises from Scripture related to your wall in the next three weeks. Beginning today you can commit to pray every morning toward the promise you are claiming. You can schedule a gathering of friends six weeks from now in anticipation of celebrating your breakthrough.

The people of our church have made bold choices that have radically transformed their home lives. For some, these at first uncomfortable choices have been the difference between romance and divorce, between obedience and rebellion, between faith and fear. But no place have these breakthroughs made a greater impact than in the lives of families who have made these principles the foundation of their homes. In fact, the idea of experiencing a breakthrough that doesn't impact home life doesn't really make sense. How can we really believe God and his promises but exclude them from everyday life?

But let's be honest. When it comes to home life, not everyone has grown up with a positive model of someone committed to making Faith Breakthroughs. In fact, some people have grown up in environments so dysfunctional, or even evil, that they assume they have no choice but to do the negative things they've seen.

## A PROMISE CHOSEN AND A LEGACY CHANGED

Let's look at a biblical example of a young man who made an incredibly courageous choice in spite of the longest of long-shot odds.

Josiah was one of the rulers of the southern kingdom of Judah during Israel's divided monarchy. At that time, the reign was passed from father to son, generation after generation.

Before looking at Josiah's life and choice, it's interesting to look at what the two kings before him chose. That would be his grandfather Manasseh and father, Amon. Their stories can be found in 2 Kings 21, where we read a synopsis of his grandfather's life first:

> Manasseh was twelve years old when he became
> king, and he reigned in Jerusalem fifty-five years. . . .
> He did what was evil in the LORD's sight, following
> the detestable practices of the pagan nations that
> the LORD had driven from the land ahead of the
> Israelites. (2 Kings 21:1-2)

Already it's pretty obvious that this man made some terrible choices. It began with forsaking the godly reign of his father, the righteous Hezekiah, and once again setting up the sacrificial sites and altars to Baal, the false god of the Canaanites. Talk about turning the clock back to horrible times!

But then Manasseh's choices became even worse:

> Manasseh also sacrificed his own son in the fire. He
> practiced sorcery and divination, and he consulted with

mediums and psychics. He did much that was evil in
the LORD's sight, arousing his anger. (2 Kings 21:6)

"Arousing [the Lord's] anger." I would think so! Manasseh's
reign was characterized by wholesale wickedness, including
child sacrifice.

So that's what Josiah's grandfather was like. Unfortunately,
as too often happens, Manasseh's son looked at his father, and
when it was his turn to rule, he kept walking in the same
horrible direction:

Amon was twenty-two years old when he became
king, and he reigned in Jerusalem two years. . . .
He did what was evil in the LORD's sight, just as his
father, Manasseh, had done. (2 Kings 21:19-20)

One problem with evil people is that they hang around
other evil people. You may have noticed that while Manasseh
reigned fifty-five years as king, Amon reigned only two years
because, the Scripture tells us, his servants plotted an assas-
sination and killed him in his own house.

So, with the king murdered, it was now Josiah's turn to
walk in the deep footprints that his grandfather and father had
walked in before him. In all likelihood, Josiah was at home
when his father was slaughtered, right in the royal palace.

With all the sin and sickness he had seen in his young life,
imagine what would be written about Josiah by the vast majority of today's sociologists, psychologists, and social scientists.
I'm pretty sure they would capture Josiah's life story in this
way: "And Josiah walked in the ways of his father, Amon, and

he did as much evil, and more, than his father and grandfather had done . . . but he didn't really have a choice."

If a sociologist today looked at Josiah's background—especially factoring in things like child sacrifice, witchcraft and the occult, murder, and more—the historic trauma and emotional abuse this poor boy suffered was enough to lead anyone to a life of evil like his ancestors. But amazingly, that is not how this story ends. Josiah made a choice that changed his legacy forever. He chose God's promises over living life behind the Walls of Sinful Living, Arrogance, and Excuses about Ancestry. Let's read his choice in the actual words of Scripture:

> Josiah was eight years old when he became king, and he reigned in Jerusalem thirty-one years. His mother was Jedidah, the daughter of Adaiah from Bozkath. He did what was pleasing in the LORD's sight and followed the example of his ancestor David. He did not turn away from doing what was right. (2 Kings 22:1-2)

Do you notice a difference between this lineage and the last one? Amon walked in the ways of his father, Manasseh. But Josiah did not walk in the ways of his father. Josiah's dad had also had an incredibly evil father. But Josiah made a profoundly bold choice about his ancestry.

He chose a different father: "He did what was pleasing in the LORD's sight and followed the example of his ancestor David."

In fact, the word used here for "ancestor" means "father" in the original text. Here was a young man who made a godly choice to pattern his life after a godly, surrogate father, a man named David, who not only walked in the ways of the Lord, but who also wrote about them in Scripture! Josiah chose to follow in the footsteps of the psalmist King David.

Footsteps like these:

Now I stand on solid ground, and I will publicly praise the LORD. (Psalm 26:12)

And these:

Teach me your ways, O LORD, that I may live according to your truth! Grant me purity of heart, so that I may honor you. (Psalm 86:11)

And these:

Make me walk along the path of your commands, for that is where my happiness is found. (Psalm 119:35)

These are all passages from the book of Psalms, revealing David's mind-set in his life—and the mind-set that Josiah, who modeled himself on David, sought to replicate.

That choice is incredibly important to understand as we continue to look at our own walls and how God's promises pave the path toward our breakthrough.

No matter your background . . . no matter what you've been through . . . no matter how many terrible things you've seen or lived through or been exposed to—*you still have a choice.* A choice to walk in godly footsteps. A choice to lay claim to God's promises. A choice to see your walls fall down, regardless of how hopeless the "experts" might say the situation is.

Still not convinced? Still not buying that God's Word and promises can reset the direction of your life, not with what you've been through, not with a wall as high as yours?

Then I'd ask you to read one more story about choice in even the most difficult of situations.

## DANCING IN FRONT OF A DEVIL

On May 22, 1944, sixteen-year-old Edith Eva Eger, along with her mother and sister, were inside a cattle car filled with Jews. The train pulled up to a siding just outside the walls of Auschwitz. As they were ordered from the railroad car, Josef Mengele himself was standing there! Mengele was already infamous as a doctor who performed inhuman experiments on people in the Nazi concentration camps.

As they were ordered from the railroad car, Mengele stood and pointed at people. He directed some to one line, others to another. Edith's mother was sent to the left line, and she and her sister to the right. Edith followed her mother, but Mengele stopped her. "Your mother is going to take a shower," he told her, turning her back to the other line.

Sometime later Edith asked a woman guard when she would see her mother again. The guard pointed to one of the gas chambers where smoke was curling into the air. "She's burning there now. Now you can talk about your mother in the past tense."

That moment was forever etched in young Edith's memory. So, too, was the memory of another terrible evening. Edith had been a ballerina. Someone discovered this, and one night she was brought before Mengele and ordered to dance for him.

When she finished, Mengele dismissed her with a small piece of bread—bread from the hand of the man responsible for killing her mother and so many others she had known.

Edith spent nearly a year at Auschwitz before being transferred to a work camp (which most assuredly saved her life). But deep down inside, where memories and walls hide, she was still a prisoner of her past. It was not until she finally took an honest look back that she began to grieve.

"I grieve over the childhood I never had," she said years later. "I grieve over the fact that I danced for Dr. Mengele in Auschwitz. I grieve that I was beaten so severely that I couldn't dance anymore."

What prompted Edith to process more deeply the traumas she experienced? Years later, after she had moved from Germany to New York City, she was asked to be a consultant on a stage play. The play was about the Holocaust, but the focus of the play was on painful relationships.

After seeing the play, she commented to reporters, "I feel it is important for everyone to see this play so they can go home and liberate themselves from their own concentration camps and to know that they have choices."

There's that word: *choices*.

She went on to say, "Many people today feel they have no choices. But even in Auschwitz we had choices."[9]

*Even in Auschwitz we had choices.*

If Holocaust survivors like Edith had choices in Auschwitz, then you and I also have choices, even in the most abominable conditions, even with the most abhorrent memories.

In the cattle car on the way to Auschwitz, Edith's mother had told her that no one could take from her what she put in her head. What you and I put in our heads is a *choice*. What will it be? Hatred or love? Bitterness or kindness? Vengeance or forgiveness?

Josiah chose to follow a different father. Edith chose to move forward in spite of her memories. And now it's your choice—that is, if you're serious about tearing down walls. So, it's time to make a choice.

It's a choice to take the time to discover God's promises that apply to your wall. And it's a choice to trust in those promises in spite of what has happened in the past or what is happening now in the present. It's a choice to allow God and his Word to break down your walls.

Will you make that choice? Today?

If I could stand beside you as you read these words, as a pastor and friend, I'd put my hand on your shoulder and pray for you:

> *Oh, gracious heavenly Father, thank you so much that you were there every time I felt so alone. That you are there when I've failed and during those times when I've felt so . . . ordinary. Thank you for standing closer than my shadow and for caring far more than anyone else ever could. And thank you, Lord, for choices. Lord, help my friend right now, today, to choose a promise that you've written just for him or her. Help my friend hear your words and claim the power you've put in your Word to tear down walls. To experience the Faith Breakthroughs you have in store.*
>
> *Thank you for being the great Wall Breaker who conquered death and who can teach us so much about*

*life. Help my friend reading this prayer to choose free-*
*dom. To choose life. To choose a different mother or*
*father like Josiah did if necessary. And to choose and*
*believe that the future can be better than the past*
*because of your love.*

*And most of all, Lord, help this precious one choose*
*you, and in the days to come, as his or her most dif-*
*ficult, most challenging wall goes down—replaced by*
*your love and light—help my friend to be a light to*
*others still caught behind a wall by sharing a promise*
*with them. Amen.*

## DISCUSSION QUESTIONS

1. Can you think of a time in your life when you were standing on a "ledge of truth"—as Ryan demonstrated to his congregation by rappelling down from the sanctuary's rafters—and you knew that you had to choose whether to live out your belief in a promise by stepping out in faith? What was that like, and how did your decision impact your faith?

2. In the last chapter, Ryan talked about getting to know the person of God before focusing on the promises of God. How does prayer help us do that? Do you ever find yourself focusing your prayers only on what God can give you rather than on how you can know him? What is the difference in those types of prayers?

3. As we reflect on our upbringings, we sometimes learn more about what not to do from our parents and other influential adults than what to do. Sometimes the best decision we can

make is to choose a completely different path from them. Can you think of an area where you might benefit from taking a different approach than your parents did? Can you think of a tough choice that your parents or others made that provides a great example to you?

# Debbie

## WHEN WALLS BECOME BREAKTHROUGHS

*Debbie had spent years* looking forward to her husband's finally retiring—only to receive the news that he was dying from cancer before they ever took a single retirement trip. And if the unfairness of that wasn't enough, life's storms grew even darker. Like Naomi in the Bible, in the waning days of her husband's life, they lost their only son as well. He was a dedicated police officer, carrying out his duties to protect and serve, when he was killed by one of the drunk drivers he was trying to keep off the road.

The following weeks were like a parade of funerals, questions, regrets, and heartache. On more than one occasion, Debbie and her surviving daughter would cry together and simply ask God, "Why?" But answers were slow to come, and all of the decisions that had to be made kept them moving forward. I had the honor of preaching at Debbie's husband's funeral and remember that beyond the grief, she was determined to count on God no matter what. For all of the circumstances she faced, she was convinced that his promises would never fail her.

Instead of wallowing behind Walls of Self-pity and

Confusion, Debbie got up each morning and reaffirmed her dependence upon the promises of God: That he would never leave her. That he would give her instruction and teaching in the way she should go. That he would direct her paths. She took to heart promises such as Psalm 121 and Psalm 71:19-21: "Your righteousness, O God, reaches to the highest heavens. You have done such wonderful things. Who can compare with you, O God? You have allowed me to suffer much hardship, but you will restore me to life again and lift me up from the depths of the earth. You will restore me to even greater honor and comfort me once again."

And God answered her prayers. Today, Debbie is an active member of our congregation, helping others overcome their own walls. She is sharing God's promises with others as the leader of a Sunday morning ladies' Bible study, and she can provide testimony that only someone who has been through her experiences is qualified to offer.

In a recent conversation with Debbie, she shared the reason she was able to continue despite all the heartache: "Don't misunderstand, grief is hard, very hard. It does not end. I miss my son and husband every day. I miss what should have been, what could have been. But I know without a doubt that I will be with them again and look forward to that day! Amen! Trusting God and leaning on his promises is all any of us can do, regardless of the situation."

Debbie experienced a test to her faith like few others I've ever met. But in the midst of her grief, God's promises enabled her to hang on.

(chapter nine)

# A PROMISE SHARED

Because we live in a culture that encourages us to keep things to ourselves and hide our weaknesses and past hurts, many of us have forgotten—or have never learned—that promises were made to be discovered and lived and then to be shared with others. The Hebrew people of Jesus' day were very intentional about following God's commands to share festivals, milestones, miracles, and memories. In fact, the Jewish nation around the world continues to lead the way in carrying on strong traditions that serve to remind one another of the promises of their history. It's time for people who are serious about breaking through to rediscover this lost art form.

## VICTORIES ARE MADE TO BE SHARED

It was a game for the ages. Even if you didn't follow basket-ball, the 1991 NBA Eastern Conference Championship at the Palace in Auburn Hills, Michigan, was must-see TV. That's because it starred none other than Michael Jordan and the Chicago Bulls on one side, as they fought to break through their chief nemesis and the defending champs. The "Bad Boy" Detroit Pistons' twin defensive hammers, Bill Laimbeer and Dennis Rodman, anchored an intimidating crew led by Joe Dumars and Isiah Thomas. It was the irre-sistible offensive force of the Bulls, meeting the immovable defensive object that was the Pistons. And I wasn't watching it on TV—I was there!

Not just *there*, but somehow my father had gotten us great seats for what turned out to be the deciding fourth game. The stadium was packed, and the game was as intense as advertised. We were all sitting on the edge of our seats until the middle of the fourth quarter, when it became fairly clear that the mighty Bulls were going to move past their greatest rivals. The Pistons had realized the same thing, and the home-team Detroit fans filed dejectedly toward the exits.

Throughout the game, my father and some friends who were with us kept commenting on the clothes I'd picked to wear to the game. As a Michael Jordan fan, I wanted the Bulls to win. But as an outsider in the opposing gym, I also wanted to get out alive. So in a personal compromise, I had worn a red button-down shirt (Bulls colors) and blue Dockers pants (Pistons colors). The reason everyone kept commenting on my choice of clothing was that I was dressed *exactly* like all the ushers at the Palace that afternoon!

And so with just five minutes left in the game, my father encouraged me to try something fun. "Ryan, just walk down the stairs and see how close you can get to the court. No one will stop you. I'm telling you, you look exactly like one of the ushers!"

I rarely get accused of being shy, so I grabbed my camera and started walking down the stairs, toward the court where the game was still being played. With each step toward the arena floor, I kept waiting for someone to step in front of me, to ask for my credentials and tell me to head back to my seat.

But to my amazement, each time I arrived at the start of another section, the usher in charge of that area would just nod and wave me through! Down through the really expensive seats and right onto the floor behind the benches. Perhaps people thought I was there to work security, because when the final buzzer sounded, I was standing on the end of the court, right by the tunnel where the coaches and players were celebrating! I was right in the middle of it!

I had a camera with me, but I had to snap my pictures without placing it up to my face. I couldn't blow my cover. So I got some incredible snapshots of MJ, Scottie Pippen, Horace Grant, and others with only half of their faces in the frame.

Just because of my mix-and-match wardrobe choice, I got to be in on the celebration of one of the most historic teams in basketball lore—at the very moment when they broke through the barrier that had haunted them for years. I got a glimpse at what happens when a wall comes down and the victory is shared among those who have journeyed together.

There are actually some significant parallels between the joy and exhilaration on that court and what a promise shared is all about. In the same way that Chicago fans couldn't stop cheering, there is a powerful sense of joy when we see almighty God break down walls in our lives. It's something we love to share, a reminder of what God has done in our lives. It's inviting people to come down courtside and celebrate with us as we lift up the Lord!

I promise I'll stop with the sports analogies, but they are a good way to highlight the excitement that comes with sharing something that's been extremely meaningful to someone, and sharing promises is a key element we've built into the culture of our church.

At Bannockburn, we encourage people at every age level to rejoice together in a Faith Breakthrough they have made. Whether a junior high student or one of our senior adults, people are encouraged to share and celebrate what God has done and is doing in their lives.

For example, we honor our high school graduates each spring with a wonderful commemoration of a promise shared. During the course of the spring semester, we offer a special Conviction Breakthrough course for those seniors to help them understand the primary worldviews they will encounter when they leave home, the differences between those worldviews and the Bible, and why they can have confidence in God's Word. On that graduation Sunday, we acknowledge those who trained for the Conviction Breakthrough with a special honor cord similar to those given for student awards. Their Walls of Doubt or Confusion may come later (during that freshman philosophy class, perhaps), but the students will already be prepared with the promises necessary to move past the walls.

A second way we encourage people to share their Faith Breakthrough is through baptism, which is the most timeless picture in the church of a promise shared. In every case, the goal is the same: to give a visual and special reminder to others of what the Lord has done and will do.

As word has spread, we have had the privilege of teaching other churches how to do the same thing through Faith Breakthrough church leader workshops. Much of that training is simply telling the stories of what has happened in the lives of our people. There is no more credible teacher than someone who has lived the power of a breakthrough.

You might wonder why Jesus said more than once to different people, "Go, and tell no one" after he healed them. Does that command contradict the power of sharing our promises? No. Whenever Jesus said those words, he wanted people to focus on his message, and he wanted to be sensitive to the timing of that message. Later, after Jesus' resurrection and ascension, the disciples were to go and tell the *world* what he had promised and done!

In other words, it is right and good to celebrate and even to memorialize what God has done in our lives. Joshua was asked to set up a memorial after God's people had marched through the Jordan River, a wall of water keeping the Israelites from the Promised Land. Likewise, memories of a promise shared leave a lasting impact of an event that may have only lasted a moment. Markers of a promise shared are more common than you think. You see them in the baptism of a renewed life, the wedding of a couple with new rings on their fingers, and a family's dedication of a child.

## WHEN EVERYDAY MOMENTS BECOME PROMISES SHARED

When we were coming up on Lily's first birthday, we all knew that this milestone meant more than just a year had passed. For her, a year of life meant that she had beaten the odds and God had answered many prayers. We wanted to celebrate more than just the anniversary of her arrival. We also knew this was an opportunity to remind ourselves, and the hundreds of friends who had prayed for our little girl, that God had kept his promises. He had never left us. In fact, his hand had brought her through more trials and challenges than most people experience in a lifetime.

We tried to think of a fitting tribute, and Lana had a great idea. Rather than hosting the average birthday party, we asked everyone to forgo bringing presents and instead to bring a gift for the Ronald McDonald House, an organization we had learned to appreciate more than we could have ever imagined. We also captured the memories on paper and film that day with a roaming video camera and actually captured many of the comments, prayers, and encouraging words through our online blog. We wanted to hold on to those testimonies so that years later we could sit down and share with her the miracle of her life.

As was only fitting for Lily's party, we actually had to postpone it a week because she was hospitalized. But when it happened, I can't begin to describe how amazing it was to be around all those people who had prayed so long and so diligently for healing. We had the opportunity to say thank you and to voice before all of those people some of the promises that had carried us through the year that had just gone by.

Milestones and anniversaries that are already a routine part of life can often become a natural and profound part of your Faith Breakthrough. Birthdays, retirement parties, Christmas celebrations, Thanksgiving meals, weddings, first days of school, and anything else you can think of can be transformed into incredible opportunities to share with others the promises that have become a part of your Faith Breakthrough.

> *Milestones and anniversaries that are already a routine part of life can often become a natural and profound part of your Faith Breakthrough.*

## SHARING YOUR BREAKTHROUGH STORY— SCARS AND ALL

Let me share a story about something I carry around with me every day. I got it the day I was preparing to go hunting with my father-in-law. I hadn't been hunting since I was young, so I borrowed one of his guns—a .30-06—and went to a local shooting range for the first time. What a mix of testosterone and gunpowder! They put you in a booth next to similar booths facing a long tunnel with targets at the end. I could tell right away that this was going to be fun. Everyone else in the room besides me was shooting handguns—weapons that, while powerful, made more of a cap-gun sound, at least with the ear protection we were wearing.

But not my rifle. When I fired it the first time, it sounded like an explosion. And every shot I took grabbed the attention of everyone in the building, like a cannon announcing its presence on the battlefield.

Shooting a deer rifle isn't rocket science. You look in the scope and place the target in the crosshairs. And shooting a gun was like riding a bike for me; I hadn't done it for years, but the principles came back pretty quickly. After two or three successful shots, I thought I might as well have some fun. After all, you never know when you might have to get more creative in the deer blind. So I took a shot while kneeling down. Then I fired a round like a soldier hiding behind a barricade, with my back against the wall and the gun barrel facing to my side. And each time I got the same result: bull's-eye!

But that's when my confidence got ahead of my wisdom, and I did something that I've wished I could do over ever since. Do you remember in the old westerns when John Wayne would take a few shots from his six-shooter? And when he was out of bullets, he'd grab his rifle and hold it up like a handgun and shoot it? Well, it turns out this only works in the movies. One of the foundations of gun safety is that when you shoot a gun, there is going to be a "kick"—a reverse impact from the force of the bullet leaving the rifle. And if the gun isn't secured against your shoulder, it's still going to blast backward.

The instant I pulled the trigger for that fateful shot, the bullet went one way and the scope of that rifle slammed right back into my forehead. *Wham!* Blood poured down my face. Of course, the audience I had created with the volume—and creativity—of my shots was enjoying the entire saga. As much as I tried to conceal the severity of the wound, the bleeding gave it away. I carefully put the gun away and headed for the checkout counter, deftly dabbing a Kleenex on my open wound. But I couldn't ignore the smirks of everyone in the store, which finally turned to laughter when the clerk offered, "Would you like a Band-Aid for that, cowboy?"

I ended up with ten stitches later that afternoon—and a half-moon scar between my eyes that I'll carry the rest of my life.

I wouldn't wish a permanent facial scar for anyone else, but it's really not so bad. As the years have passed, it has been fun to share the story. I can't tell you how many people I've met who made the same mistake!

*Sharing your breakthrough blesses those around you who need to break down their own walls.*

I tell that story because there is something about scars that leads to sharing. The story of your scars may be difficult to tell, but it may be the very thing it takes to help others move past their own hurts and challenges. Part of sharing your story is to firmly establish the breakthrough in your own life, but sharing is also a blessing to those around you who need to break down their own walls as well. When we're willing to share our scars, we open the door for real healing in the lives of those around us—as well as in our own.

## DON'T WAIT TO SHARE!

You don't have to be miles beyond your wall to share. In fact, it can be a trap to think you have to have everything resolved before you let others in on what God is doing in your life. You can—and should—celebrate your very first blow to the wall! Sharing with others while you're still on the journey gives weight to the decisions you are making, and it allows others to cheer you on as you experience the breakthrough.

Statistics tell us that people are always more successful at an exercise program when they have a workout partner. The reason is fairly simple: we don't want to let someone else down, and we're motivated to keep going when we realize that our partner is counting on our keeping our word. Sharing our breakthroughs works the same way: it builds momentum toward the victory, even in the early stages of the process.

Choosing to share early in the process is important for another reason: there will be a day when the challenges grow harder, and you're going to need the conviction that there is no turning back. Indeed, the times of testing will be just the thing to solidify your breakthrough.

## DISCUSSION QUESTIONS

1. Describe a time when you witnessed something so special taking place that the people around you felt compelled to celebrate it—perhaps even spontaneously. What made it so important to come together and share that victory?

2. Some of our greatest opportunities to share with others come out of our most difficult experiences. Why is it, then, that we are often so tempted to keep those stories to ourselves— even when God has given us victory over them?

3. Brainstorm some ways that people who have experienced breakthroughs could share those victories with others. How might you use one of those ways to let others know about a breakthrough in your own life?

# Duke & Angie
## WHEN WALLS BECOME BREAKTHROUGHS

*Duke and Angie were* raising a wonderful family and cruising through life. Their faith in God was a steady, if not convenient, one. Unlike others in this book, they enjoyed much of what we would normally hope for in the context of the American dream and even matched the description of ideal church members. But in the midst of what was seen, there were invisible walls.

Duke recently shared with me that he had fallen into a trap with which most of us are familiar: the constant quest for success, for the next big thing, and for the "stuff" that came with it. This empty journey had completely turned his priorities upside down, and he was working diligently to obtain things with no lasting substance—even while he was unknowingly building barriers that were robbing him of all that really mattered in his life.

In one terrible evening, he almost lost all that mattered in just one phone call. It was the kind of call we all dread receiving: Angie and the two children had traveled to Lubbock, Texas, to visit her parents. Angie, the kids, and her parents were in their Suburban when they were hit head-on by an oncoming car. A few seconds of exploding sheet metal and flying glass had demanded the ultimate price for some in the vehicle. When Duke received the phone call that evening, the hospital representative could tell him only that his family had been involved in an accident with fatalities, and that there were two in the Suburban who had not survived. All the rest were being rushed to the hospital, and the caller didn't know which passengers were still alive.

When Duke hung up the phone, he fell to his knees and cried out to God: *Lord, please spare my family! Please save my family!* Some time later he learned the two children had arrived at the hospital and were going to make it. Now he had the somber anticipation of which of the remaining three had survived.

Moments seemed like hours.

And finally the call came. Angie was alive, but both of her parents had died in the accident. If it's possible to feel relief with the news that loved ones have passed away, this was the case. In the midst of his grief for the loss of his in-laws, Duke was fully aware that God had given him a brand-new opportunity to reorder his life.

With his entire family in the hospital several hours' drive from home, he arranged for a pilot to fly his private plane to Lubbock. He still remembers frantically packing for a hospital stay of who-knew-how-long and the lonely drive to the airport. The arrival at the airport brought more bad news. Severe thunderstorms shook the sky almost the entire way to Lubbock. The plane was large enough to be radar equipped, but that didn't guarantee they could make it all the way to their destination without having to divert the flight, and that hardly seemed like a viable option given his desperation to be with the ones he loved most. Duke prayed some more in the plane, and prayers were lifted all over the state as word spread about the horrible accident. Duke recalls how strongly he could sense those prayers and the presence and power of God with them.

The approach to Lubbock became more and more unlikely as the night wore on. Radar showed the most dangerous storms imaginable all around them. Duke and his pilot witnessed lightning flashing on both sides of the plane like great walls of angry, explosive clouds. Yet somehow, remarkably, a narrow path of clear skies remained in front of the plane. Duke recalled his pilot saying numerous times, "Hang on, in another thirty miles things are going to get rough!" But they would fly another thirty miles, and the skies would continue to open. All the way to Lubbock, with storms raging around them, there was not so much as a bump in their flight. Sixty seconds after they landed cleanly in Lubbock and got into their car, the sky began to pour sheets of rain.

In those moments, Duke felt the strong sense that God's hand had not left him or his family and that his Savior would never leave him. That assurance carried the family through the challenging days of recovery, through the difficult memorial services, and into the first few days when all was supposed to be back to normal.

But as the days went by, it became apparent that "normal" would never be the same. Duke and Angie no longer wanted to experience life as usual. God's promises had broken down their Wall of Misplaced Priorities. They felt strongly that the

Lord had given them another chance to rewrite their legacy, and they were not about to let it pass by.

Duke's business as a custom home builder remains as strong as ever, but it is no longer what all else revolves around. He lives by God's promise in Matthew 6:33, which instructs us to "seek the Kingdom of God above all else, and live righteously, and he will give you everything you need." His passion for his Lord not only grows stronger every day, but it overflows into the lives of his wife and children. Angie serves on our prayer team at church, with a new understanding of prayer's power. Not only has Duke caught the vision for what it means to claim God's promises regarding passing a legacy to his children, he now teaches a class to other dads in the church who are taking the same strong challenge. Every day has become a gift, a gift custom-designed for a life of Faith Breakthroughs.

Duke and Angie know what it means to overcome walls through the power of the Faith Breakthrough. What's more, they have experienced the significance of a promise shared—and how it can change not only our lives, but others' lives as well.

# chapter ten

# THE TEST: WHERE BREAKTHROUGHS HAPPEN

We can talk endlessly about verses and mind-sets and examples and Faith Breakthroughs. But there will come that time—that test—when we'll either use God's promise to face up to our walls or retreat into defeat. For me that time came with a scream from the other side of our house. . . .

I mentioned in chapter 1 that our youngest daughter, Lily, was born with significant health challenges. She remained a guest at the hospital a bit longer than most newborns due to some breathing concerns, but when we brought her home for the first time, we felt confident that any dangers were behind us and expected to begin the regular routine of life with a baby. Five days later came the terrible night I still remember vividly.

I was in our bedroom when I heard my mother-in-law,

Nita, scream my name from Lily's room across the hall. I raced toward her cries. As I ran in, Nita was hovering over our daughter, who was already blue and looked lifeless. I began rescue breathing as Lana called 911. We prayed and cried and performed CPR and begged God to bring help soon and to save our little girl.

By the time EMS arrived, Lily was breathing again, but the evidence of all that was wrong inside her heart would render each day to follow very different from the ones before.

That was the first time we almost lost Lily, but not the last. And each time was like coming face-to-face with the walls that Lana and I were quietly building. All our worries and fears and anxieties and doubts were becoming walls, brick by brick, between us and the Lord, a God we had always known to be loving and kind, but whose strategy in these moments we could not comprehend.

I would be lying if I said that the testing we have faced through Lily's life is now something we can rejoice over, but I can honestly say that amazing things have happened in the face of those tests. Lana and I have had to cling to God's promises in ways we never knew before. Promises that he would "never leave [us] nor forsake [us]" (from Hebrews 13:5, NKJV) or our baby Lily. He has not left, even as we continue to face those tests that bring us right back to our walls—and right back to God's promises that break them down again.

The truth of the matter may be something none of us wants to hear: no breakthrough is complete until the testing comes. In fact, this is where the three steps of discovering, choosing, and sharing God's promises come together to form the weapon that finally overcomes the wall.

The testing is the proving ground of the breakthrough. It is the fire that forges the separate elements into the steel strong enough to break down walls.

Sometimes passages become so familiar that we forget their incredible power. For example, James 1:2-3 has been quoted time and again: "Dear brothers and sisters, when troubles come your way, consider it an opportunity for great joy. For you know that when your faith is tested, your endurance has a chance to grow."

> *The testing is the proving ground of the breakthrough. It is the fire that forges the separate elements into the steel strong enough to break down walls.*

We have learned over the years of Lily's struggles how true this verse is when we trust. It is never easy, but it is always true.

Yes, it is the nature of walls to grow larger and more fearsome during difficult times. But it is also the nature of God to show us a way through anything we face and to lead us to the life we need and want.

Certainly Lana and I aren't alone in facing a test that leads to a breakthrough. You've already read the stories of several wall breakers from our church who have faced the testing and broken through. And like them, there was a man in the Bible with a very unusual name who did the same thing.

## AN AMAZING PICTURE OF A FAITH BREAKTHROUGH

Habakkuk lived in 620 BC, but his story sounds like it is right out of headline news. Habakkuk and the people he was leading were confused about the challenging times they were facing. In fact, at the beginning of his book, Habakkuk lists six things that he simply couldn't figure out.

Sit in front of your television tonight, click over to a local or national news channel, and tell me if this doesn't sound like what's happening in the world. Wherever Habakkuk looked, he saw sin, wickedness, destruction, and violence. He saw no justice in the courts, and everywhere the wicked seemed like they outnumbered the righteous.

And there's one more thing.

Habakkuk was facing a wall because of all he saw around him. In Habakkuk 1:2, he asks, "How long, O Lord, must I call for help? But you do not listen!"

Just like we are all prone to do, when times get tough and God's plan is out of sight, the prophet of God faced a moment of testing. Habakkuk was unable to hear God, to see God, or to understand. He joined his people in wondering why God was somehow "hidden" from what was going on. In our darkest moments, we wonder whether God is even paying attention.

In Habakkuk's case, it got even worse. Habakkuk heard from God, but it was not what he wanted to hear: almighty God had just told him that things were going to get worse, not better. How's that for the opposite of a health-and-wealth message!

It's like praying that God will take away an illness a friend is facing, only to watch our friend get worse. It is in these moments when we pray and get the "wrong" answer that we face the biggest crisis in the midst of the breakthrough—and we have to choose between a breakthrough and a breakdown.

I can't see the answer. Will I still trust?

I can't understand the circumstances. Will I still believe?

I can't imagine a positive outcome. Will I still press on?

Let me make this personal for a moment. While Lily's health problems have kept us on the alert in recent years, our oldest daughter has dealt with a physical condition of her own. Ryley has struggled with type 1 diabetes since she was five years old. While this condition is not as daunting as Lily's struggles, what Ryley has faced has been tremendously challenging for her and for us as well.

As a diabetic, Ryley's life has never been free from shots and insulin pumps. We must also draw blood from our little girl multiple times *every day*. These "finger sticks" were especially trying when she was very young. It hurts to have blood taken, no matter how often it's done. I can remember praying so hard for Ryley to be healed from this disease. But a yes answer to prayer has not yet come. In fact, while she has been a trouper over the years and almost never complains, I remember vividly one really tough night when she was about six years old.

It was time to take blood, *again*, and it had hurt her, *again*, and she was crying in my arms, *again*. And then Ryley looked up at me and asked in a sad, pleading voice, "Daddy, is there going to be diabetes in heaven?"

When it's your child who's hurting, when there's no answer to your prayers that makes sense to you, when you've prayed so hard to relieve a loved one's pain—*and it gets worse?* It's easy to say at times like that, as Habakkuk did, "God, why don't you hear? God, why can't you see?" It's easy at that point for a wall to go up or to get higher—a Wall of Doubt, or Anger, or Fear, or Uncertainty.

Of course, it's easy for walls to go up in times of testing.

But there's an amazing truth about breakthroughs that involves the very same test: the tests that seem to be drawing you far from God are the very things God can use to bring down the walls in your life.

You don't have to like the tests you go through, but you must see the opportunities that they bring. Tests offer a chance to prove God's promises like nothing else on earth can do.

## A PROMISE TESTED; A PROMISE CONFIRMED

As I was writing this book, I almost changed this chapter's title to a more positive one: "A Promise Confirmed." After all, isn't that what needs to happen in the midst of a trial? But that's just the point: there is no confirmation without the testing; the two go hand in hand.

*The tests that seem to be drawing you far from God are the very things God can use to bring down the walls in your life.*

In science class, we used to have to test our hypotheses. It was only after the testing proved our theories to be true that we had confirmation. And the same is true in real life, as we see with Habakkuk. He made a clear decision in the midst of the test that absolutely transformed everything that took place from that point forward:

Even though the fig trees have no blossoms, and there are no grapes on the vines; even though the olive crop fails, and the fields lie empty and barren; even though the flocks die in the fields, and the cattle barns are empty, yet I will rejoice in the LORD! I will be joyful in the God of my salvation! The Sovereign LORD is my strength! He makes me as surefooted as a deer, able to tread upon the heights. (Habakkuk 3:17-19)

Incredible words. Put another way, Habakkuk was completely convinced that God would provide the strength he needed to blast through the walls in front of him, regardless of how circumstances worked out. And the same promises that carried him through the tests of his life can be the dawn of your own Faith Breakthrough. When put to the test, you discover that things don't have to go as planned for God's promises to be completely, unconditionally true and life-giving.

## THE DIFFERENCE BETWEEN BREAKTHROUGHS AND BREAKDOWNS

Several years ago, when we were first introducing the concept of Faith Breakthroughs to the leaders in our church, somebody said something about the process that has really resonated with me: "When you face life's walls, you really only have two choices: have a break*through* or have a break-*down!*"

Breakthroughs and breakdowns commonly have all of the same ingredients, but it is how we use those ingredients in the midst of the trial that will determine success or failure. When people break down on their way past the wall, it is never because a true promise of God failed; it is because the person in the trial failed to focus on the promise, becoming distracted by the circumstances that can be readily seen. On the other hand, like Habakkuk, a person breaks through when he fixes his eyes on the unseen promise regardless of the circumstances. In this case, the test becomes only the opportunity to prove that the promise is true!

We live in a world that is so confusing, so upsetting, so illogical, so evil, and so unfair that if we walk by sight we're headed for a breakdown. But when we walk by faith— trusting God's Word even in the midst of all we see around us—we take the first step toward a Faith Breakthrough.

The "test phase" of the breakthrough is probably not your favorite part of the book, but it may be the most critical. And the good news is this: whether or not you use your tests to experience a Faith Breakthrough, trials are going to come along anyway, so at least those tests now have a purpose.

I mentioned the testing that took place in science class, but obviously every teacher in school uses the same method. They teach the material, and then they use tests to be sure that their students have learned the subject that was taught. There's really no other way to know for sure. I had a few teachers, though, who at least made tests a little bit easier. They would either tell us in advance exactly what would be asked on the test, or they would allow us to use our notes and texts during the test-taking process. The great news about real-life testing is that God has offered us both of those advantages.

The tests of life are all "open book": we can go to the Bible and study God's promises over and over again even as we're in the midst of the test. And the tests of life are also pre-disclosed: we may not know the exact way the test will be given, but we can be assured that every test will contain the same three questions, which we will explore in the next chapter.

# DISCUSSION QUESTIONS

1. Looking back over your life, what would you say are the three most significant tests you've ever had to face?

2. Habakkuk's understanding that things were getting worse actually helped him trust God more rather than less. What is the difference between being a pessimist—expecting bad things to happen in the future—and a realistic optimist— expecting that there will be trials, but that God will still be in control?

3. Many tests we face are unique to each person, but some are universal. What are some trials that almost everybody has to face? How does it help to know that they are coming?

4. When it comes to your own times of testing, which of the three "promise steps" (a promise discovered, promise chosen, or promise shared) is hardest to take?

# David & Wendy
## WHEN WALLS BECOME BREAKTHROUGHS

*Most every girl dreams* of her wedding day and carries in her heart the hope of "happily ever after." Unfortunately, things don't always go as planned.

When David and Wendy were married, everything looked great from the outside. But Wendy didn't know that David was bringing baggage into their new home, and his secret life of pornography quietly eroded the foundation of their marriage. Even worse, this sin eventually led to more bad choices. And as is always the case, the truth eventually came to light, and Wendy's dreams of a perfect family life were destroyed.

David recently reminded me of the depth to which he had fallen:

> *My "baggage" unfortunately was much wider than pornography, as you know. It included a sexual addiction that I was powerless to defeat without God. It also led to one of the greatest regrets of my life: adultery. I forfeited the ability and the privilege of telling my three girls*

*later on in life that I had been faithful to their*
*mother. As I grow older and farther away from*
*those dark days, this is the fact that seems to*
*remain and even grow larger in my mind.*

David was humiliated and broken. Wendy felt angry and betrayed. Several friends reminded her that she had every right to pack up her daughters and walk away. After all, no one deserved the heartache she was going through.

But something else happened entirely.

David and Wendy walked through Christian counseling together, and David remained humble and repentant about all he had done. He discovered new promises from Scripture that could help him overcome the temptations that had buried him so deeply behind walls of lust and idolatry. Psalm 119:9-11 became real to him: "How can a young person stay pure? By obeying your word. I have tried hard to find you— don't let me wander from your commands. I have hidden your word in my heart, that I might not sin against you." As he let God's promise transform his heart and mind, he grew determined to love Wendy in a new and deeper way and to prove to her he would be the kind of husband she had always hoped he would be.

In the meantime, Wendy began to discover a Wall of Bitterness all her own that she hadn't previously recognized. This new understanding didn't mean that David's actions were her fault; it simply meant that she had her own places of unbelief that she was holding back from God. And until she dealt with them, she was convinced that she would never be able to allow her marriage to heal. She claimed the promise of Psalm 34:18, which states that "the Lord is close to the brokenhearted; he rescues those whose spirits are crushed." David put it this way:

> *For me to begin to move away from my sin, God had to completely break me down and thus build me back up. For Wendy to endure recovery and the overall rebirth of our marriage, she also had to allow God to break her down and thus build her back up. This process was extremely painful at the time. However, the blessings that we are experiencing today are from God! And a healthy marriage has overshadowed the pain a thousand times over.*

The healing did not come instantly, but it came nonetheless. Today, David and Wendy remain happily married and deeply committed to their God and to one another. They also lead a growing ministry through our church that helps other couples experiencing the pain and heartache that pornography inevitably brings.

In David and Wendy's story we can see so much of the breakthrough path we've been on—from needing and longing for real change, to hearing of the power of a promise, to discovering, choosing, and sharing that promise. David and Wendy have walked the path and continue today to head toward the kind of fulfilling life they never thought possible.

# chapter eleven

# THE TEST QUESTIONS

We recently reconstructed a thirty-foot section of the Berlin Wall outside our church building as a symbol of the spiritual walls people in our community are facing. It was amazing to watch passersby react to this imposing structure on the corner of a busy intersection. We even replicated the graffiti from pictures of the actual wall and invited people to come and write on the wall themselves.

In researching the dimensions for this imitation, it became apparent that we could give people a glimpse of only the West Berlin side of the Wall. The Eastern side would have been far too complicated and dangerous to re-create. In fact, the part that most of us recall seeing in pictures and on television doesn't tell even half the story.

The Wall began with a simple combination of barbed wire

and fencing, but people continued to escape to the West. As a result, a "death strip" was added on the East German side that kept people from even getting *close* to the wall. Imagine standing in East Berlin and, despite the incredible odds against success, deciding you were going to make a break for freedom in the West.

To get across the death strip in order to reach to the wall itself, you would have to climb a ten-foot-high, razor-wire fence. If you succeeded in scaling that first fence, you would then have to run across a thirty-foot-wide strip of extremely fine beach-grade sand. The sand wasn't to slow people down. It was to record any footprints they made in their flight to freedom. And it would also mark which guards were closest to the footprints, in order to punish them for not being vigilant enough to stop the person from scaling the wire wall and trying to escape in the first place.

On the other side of the sand came deep anti-vehicle trenches filled with concrete dragon's teeth big enough to stop tanks. Get through these and, as you headed toward freedom, you would run into the terrible fakir beds—wide beds of nearly eight-inch-long nails. These nail beds ran the entire length of the wall and were placed in varying clustered patterns, set at all angles. That unique angling guaranteed that no matter how carefully you walked or ran, you'd be skewered, cut, slowed down, or stopped by the long, rusted nails. If you somehow made it through the bed of nails, you would then set off a motion sensor that would sound an ear-splitting alarm while you were still fifty feet from the wall. That alarm would put on alert the closest of the 116 armed guard towers and twenty concrete bunkers built into the wall that loomed in front of you. And in that tower or bunker, twenty-four hours a day, soldiers had specific orders to kill anyone attempting a crossing. In other areas, you might face an angry German shepherd trained to stop you at all costs. And keep in mind that you would have had to do all this just to *get* to the wall, much less get over it.

In much the same way, the spiritual walls we face are not as simple to scale as they might appear at first glance. They are secured by three key obstacles that take the form of questions. If answered incorrectly or incompletely, these questions will make it very difficult to change the mind-sets that make up our walls.

## THE UNANSWERED QUESTIONS THAT HOLD US BACK

In John 14, Jesus was just hours away from his arrest, unjust trial, and crucifixion. Knowing full well the terrible events of the next few hours, Jesus gathered his most faithful followers for one last evening meal before the long-foretold events unfolded. Alone with them in the upper room, Jesus shared some of his most loving, intimate, familiar words with those he loved most deeply. And he began by giving them a promise:

> Don't let your hearts be troubled. Trust in God, and trust also in me. There is more than enough room in my Father's home. If this were not so, would I have told you that I am going to prepare a place for you? When everything is ready, I will come and get you, so that you will always be with me where I am. And you know the way to where I am going. (John 14:1-4)

When Jesus makes a promise, you can take it to the bank. And in this case, Jesus clearly laid out the timetable for what was about to take place. He was leaving, but he would come back to them. In the meantime, he would prepare a heavenly place for them to come and join him, where the only walls would be the good kind, those surrounding the new heaven and new earth, complete with mansions built especially for them.

Even so, these disciples had seen the whole world turn upside down in the few days leading up to this somber moment with their King. In their minds, it wasn't supposed to end like this. There was one disciple named Thomas who spoke up, perhaps echoing the sentiments of the others. Still, it was clear that he was fighting a growing Wall of Doubt. "'No, we don't know, Lord,' Thomas said. 'We have no idea where you are going, so how can we know the way?'" (John 14:5).

Have you ever seen a movie and then gone back a second time and seen things you'd missed? There's actually a reason why you see more with repeated viewings. It's something called layering that master filmmakers build into their movies, and it's when they put so much into a scene that moves so quickly, you simply don't see it all the first time.

Keep that strategy in mind when reading Thomas's question. At first glance, it seems like he was asking one question. But with a closer look, we discover that there are three questions layered into one.

Look again at the words of Thomas, and this time I'll slow down the film and audio track. You'll find that the three layered questions are not unlike those every one of us asks sooner or later:

- "No, we don't know, Lord," Thomas said.
- "We have no idea where you are going,
- so how can we know the way?"

*Test question 1: Who is God?*
"No, we don't know, Lord," Thomas said.

Thomas revealed through his question that he had a genuine desire to be with Jesus. He was frustrated, though, because Jesus was sharing a plan that did not match Thomas's own expectations. Thomas had been anticipating a kingly crowning, and instead his Lord was going away? Despite all of their time together, Thomas's question exhibited a genuine misunderstanding of who God truly is.

As long as the question "Who is God?" remained unanswered in Thomas's life, he was unable to move past his Wall of Doubt. It wasn't that he didn't believe in God or in Jesus as God's Son. Jesus' claims of deity weren't just made that night. Thomas had heard them time and again over the past three years. It was simply that the crisis of the moment was causing him to rethink the *nature* of the God he thought he had completely figured out.

> *The crisis of the moment was causing Thomas to rethink the nature of the God he thought he had completely figured out.*

Every person who has ever lived has faced the very same crisis and the very same question. For many of us, the question of who God is comes at a time when we *thought* we had figured him out—as if he is simply a puzzle for us to solve. And reducing God to a simple equation will always fall short. For some, he is a mysterious force known only as "a Higher

Power." For others, he is a happy-go-lucky "Man Upstairs" who is almost seen as a buddy.

When God called Moses to lead the Hebrew slaves out of Egypt, Moses encountered the Lord on an ordinary mountainside through a bush that burned but was not consumed by the fire. But ordinary surroundings aside, it became readily apparent that the God he was facing was far more than he had ever imagined: "'Do not come any closer,' the LORD warned. 'Take off your sandals, for you are standing on holy ground. I am the God of your father—the God of Abraham, the God of Isaac, and the God of Jacob'" (Exodus 3:5-6).

God was telling Moses a lot in that one statement. He was saying that he was a personal God. He desired to communicate with Moses. He was saying that he was a holy God. He was above and beyond anything Moses could imagine in terms of righteousness and goodness. He was saying that he was an eternal God. He stretched across the generations and, in fact, across all of eternity. He was saying that he was a loving God. He had been faithful through all generations.

Of course, when problems come into our lives, they often lead to confusion about the way we have defined God. The same was true of Moses. Just a few sentences away from God's profound statement regarding his identity, after he commanded Moses to go in his name, Moses found himself questioning God once again. Exodus 3:13 tells us, "But Moses protested, 'If I go to the people of Israel and tell them, "The God of your ancestors has sent me to you," they will ask me, "What is his name?" Then what should I tell them?'"

He was asking the Way Question: "Who is God, and how

can I know him?" God's response reiterated what he had already told Moses:

> God replied to Moses, "I Am Who I Am. Say this to the people of Israel: I Am has sent me to you." God also said to Moses, "Say this to the people of Israel: Yahweh, the God of your ancestors—the God of Abraham, the God of Isaac, and the God of Jacob— has sent me to you. This is my eternal name, my name to remember for all generations." (Exodus 3:14-15)

That response also echoed something very important that every person needs to understand about the critical question "Who is God?": there is only one God, he is worthy of our trust, and we don't have to fully understand him to trust him. I call this the Way Question because only when we understand who he is can we really gain access to God and his promises.

Until you get the "Who" right, you will never get the "Way" right.

It's not really the walls that keep us from fully understanding God. Our human nature does that on its own. But walls accentuate what we *don't* know about him and force our attention away from what we *do* know about him. Walls block our ability to see past the obstacles in front of us. They get us to ask, "Who is God?" in a way that, like Thomas, implies, "God, if you're not going to act according to my expectations, then how do I know I can trust you, or even if you are real?"

The longer we ask "Who is God?" without an answer, the higher our walls will grow, and the further we will feel from God's promises . . . and most importantly from God himself. The shadow of that imposing wall leaves us feeling even more hopeless. The greater the darkness, the less we can see of God's presence and the more we will struggle with the Way Question, "Who is God?"

In *The Lion, the Witch and the Wardrobe* by C. S. Lewis, Susan and Lucy prepare to meet Aslan the lion, who represents Christ. Two talking animals, Mr. and Mrs. Beaver, prepare the children for the encounter.

"Ooh," says Susan, "I'd thought he was a man. Is he—quite safe? I shall feel rather nervous about meeting a lion."

"That you will, dearie," says Mrs. Beaver. "And make no mistake, if there's anyone who can appear before Aslan without their knees knocking, they're either braver than most or else just silly."

"Then he isn't safe?" said Lucy.

"Safe?" says Mr. Beaver. "Don't you hear what Mrs. Beaver tells you? Who said anything about safe? 'Course he isn't safe. But he's good. He's the King, I tell you."[10]

Mr. Beaver knew a secret about Aslan that we would do well to know about God. We don't have to fully understand him to ace the Way Question in times of testing. It is enough to realize that he is a righteous, all-powerful God who loves us and has a plan for our lives. But that plan does not mean we will ever know all there is to know about him. We will spend our entire lives learning more and more about him, but in the meantime we have to trust that the unknowns about him include his eternal faithfulness and trustworthiness as well.

The closer we get to the answer of the Way Question—"Who is God?"—the more in awe we will be of him. And the closer we'll come to a Faith Breakthrough.

### *Test question 2: What is true?*

Just hours after Jesus spoke to the disciples in John 14, he stood before the Roman governor Pilate, who asked him, "What is truth?" (John 18:38).

Earlier in the upper room, Thomas was expressing this same issue when he said, "We have no idea where you are going, so how can we know the way?" (John 14:5).

Layered into that inquiry is a question that always comes with trials and tests—one that I call the Truth Question: "What is true?" Tests have a tendency to bring with them incredible confusion. We think we know one thing, but the rules and reality seem to change.

We have a GPS in one of our cars that is several years old, and I have been too cheap to pay for the updated subscription. As a result, many of the newer roads and subdivisions near our home are not included on the maps. We have often found ourselves driving along, when suddenly the map just ends and we are driving across blank space, according to the car display, and we really have no way of knowing which way to go. That's how life can be when we lose sight of the directional understanding found in God's Word, when suddenly our circumstances contradict what we expected, or hoped, would be reality.

In the first hours after the Berlin Wall went up, confusion was the one emotion that reigned supreme according to almost every eyewitness account. Simple questions ruled the day:

- How will we get to our favorite park that was just a few blocks away but now lies behind a wall?

- How will we communicate with our loved ones
  with all East-West telephone lines now severed?
- Will the Western powers come to our rescue, and
  why haven't they come yet?

The early stages of a test tend to replace certainty with confusion. To force us to redraw the map. To twist what we know to be true and to call it false.

Thomas had just heard the promise that Jesus would be leaving and that he would return someday. But Thomas completely ignored the promises and cut to the confusion: "Lord, we have no idea where you are going."

Not only do we second-guess who God is in these moments, we also begin to ask even more disturbing questions: If God is righteous, all-powerful, all-knowing, compassionate, and gracious, then why can't he solve my problem? Why do good people suffer? Why does it seem like the justice due me escapes God's notice?

Walls get us to ask, "God, if you're really a loving God, where's the justice? Why don't you act to relieve my pain?"

Or as Lana and I have asked too many times when our child struggled for life and our walls grew higher, "God, we know that you are able to heal. So how could you let this continue happening to our child?"

Have you ever looked at the world's injustice and questioned God's love, reality, and willingness to act? It is terribly hard for veterans to come home from foreign wars and not ask the question, "God, why did that man die and I came home alive?" or, "God, if our cause is right, then why did I or my friend have to suffer?"

As a pastor, I have encountered people who have almost drowned themselves in life's toughest questions. They have thrown away years of joy simply because they refuse to accept that God can be good and yet allow the tragedies they have seen or experienced. But when those same people begin to dwell on God's promises as the truths they will live by, things begin to change. When Faith Breakthroughs come, suddenly the same question that hindered them becomes a part of their victory!

And remember, there's a third question that walls bring up in our lives. I call it the Life Question.

### Test question 3: "Why am I here?"

Let's review Thomas's question one more time: "'No, we don't know, Lord,' Thomas said. 'We have no idea where you are going, so how can we know the way?'" (John 14:5).

It seems that Thomas deeply desired to understand, to believe with conviction the words of his Leader. But he was stuck on what he was supposed to do next. His rationale was simple:

- My understanding of my Lord has been challenged.
- My recognition of what *should be* (and what I would do if I were him) no longer makes sense to me.

Which leads to a final conclusion:

- If I cannot count on my God or his promises,
  how can I possibly count on his plan for my life?

When we get to the Life Question, what stumps us is the purpose behind the steps we are taking. Like the East

Berliner who made it past the outer barriers, this last nagging question can hold us back even once we've started the process of discovering, choosing, and sharing God's promises.

When you begin to see walls come down in your life, a whole new world of opportunities will open up to you. Remember the story of Brad in chapter 1? He struggled with addiction to prescription drugs for years before God's promises completely tore down his wall. He has learned to possess promises of God's fulfillment and satisfaction, of the power to overcome temptation, and of the joy he has in Christ. Of course, he is extremely grateful that he has moved beyond this terrible barrier, but he now faces the test of filling that old passion in his life with the things God intends—of getting on the path of purpose for which he was designed. I have found that people who overcome addiction but simply dwell on what used to be without filling their lives with new goals are in grave danger of falling backward.

I know of few people who have not wrestled with this key question of life: "Why am I here?" In my early adulthood I thought my calling was to sing and write Christian music, only to see the doors close over and over. I realized later that God had something far better in mind. But during those days before it made sense that God had a different plan than my own, the Life Question lingered and threatened to paralyze my mind-set, my family, and my ministry.

The word often translated "life" in the New Testament is *zoë*. That word literally means "movement." Things that have life are things that move. And one thing walls are perfectly suited to do is to block movement. Things that aren't moving are dying. In short, part of what walls represent is the opposite of life.

That may be the best summary of what's at stake in answering these three foundational questions: We can answer wrongly and suffer the inevitable separation from all that could be. Or we can answer correctly and keep moving toward all that God intended us to be.

## NO ONE ESCAPES THE THREE QUESTIONS

In the studio where I used to work, there was a sink. Above the sink was a mirror. I stopped at this place several times each day to tidy up and look at myself in the mirror. Alongside the mirror was a photograph of the troublesome old woman.[11]

That is a quote from Robert Fulghum, author of the best-selling book *All I Really Need to Know I Learned in Kindergarten*. And that "troublesome old woman" he writes about is Mother Teresa. The occasion of the photograph was her acceptance speech of the Nobel Peace Prize in Oslo, Norway, on December 11, 1979.

"Each time I looked in the mirror at myself," writes Fulghum, "I also looked at her face. In it I have seen more than I can tell; and from what I saw, I understood more than I can say."

That is the power of looking at someone whose life was fully sold out to Christ. On that day in Oslo, Mother Teresa stood all of four feet, eleven inches tall, and wore her signature blue-bordered sari and worn leather sandals.

(She was wearing a sari and sandals in spite of the below-zero weather in Norway because that was the uniform of her Missionaries of Charity order and the only clothes she owned.)

In her acceptance speech, her words were exactly what we would have expected from a modern-day saint like her. They were words full of warmth as she reminded the world of the upcoming Christmas holidays and that "radiating joy," joy that's shared with others, "is real." She challenged to action all who listened, saying, "It is not enough for us to say: I love God, but I do not love my neighbor." She shared her love for Jesus in pointing out that by his death on the cross, God made himself "the hungry one—the naked one—the homeless one." And she concluded that everywhere Christians go, "Christ [should be] in our hearts, Christ in the poor that we meet, Christ in the smile that we give and the smile that we receive."

Now *that's* the kind of speech we'd expect from a wall breaker, the kind of words we'd expect from a woman whom no one would seriously question as being sold-out to her Savior. Someone who spent decades breaking down caste-system walls in Calcutta from the day she started walking across the street to pick up poor, dying people and taking in AIDS-infected orphans. Someone whose words and actions broke down the Wall of Indifference to the suffering of untouchables worldwide and who motivated millions of people to do more for others as they sought to live out Christ's love.

Surely if there was a person who didn't have to worry about spiritual and emotional walls in his or her life, it was that "troublesome old woman," the one who experienced and shared so much of God's love with the poor and the world.

But if that's what you think about Mother Teresa, you're mistaken.

Less than three months before her acceptance speech, in a letter written to a spiritual confidant that was released after her death, Mother Teresa wrote with unvarnished honesty about Walls of Doubt, Loneliness, and Emptiness in her life.

"Jesus has a very special love for you," Mother Teresa assured the Rev. Michael Van Der Peet with whom she was corresponding. "As for me, the silence and the emptiness is so great that I look and do not see, listen and do not hear."

Read that again, and realize those words are coming from arguably one of the most godly people who ever walked the planet as she described a Wall of Emptiness she faced.

In other letters, she wrote with incredible honesty of dryness, darkness, and loneliness. In one letter, she shared openly how she felt like a hypocrite after giving a talk about experiencing Jesus' love at a time when she felt he was far from her. "I spoke as if my very heart was in love with God—tender, personal love," she wrote. "If you were [there], you would have said, 'What hypocrisy.'"

Can you even imagine Mother Teresa at times feeling like she was a hypocrite? Someone so Christlike, facing a Wall of Doubt in her life, just like we do so often?

I hope you can. Because that's another thing about the nature of walls: they are equal-opportunity oppressors. Equal-opportunity barriers that can make us question and doubt and fear . . . even if you're Mother Teresa.

We'd have expected famous spiritual leaders to be different

from us stuck-in-everyday-traffic saints. But if we look closer, we'll see that we all fall short. We all have to face up to the fact that with our fallen nature comes a propensity—I think a certainty—to one day face walls. Even if we're the apostle Paul:

> I know that nothing good lives in me, that is, in
> my sinful nature. I want to do what is right, but
> I can't. I want to do what is good, but I don't. I
> don't want to do what is wrong, but I do it anyway.
> (Romans 7:18-19)

I know a seminary professor who argued that Paul couldn't have written those words himself. Obviously (to this man) they must have been added much later by a meddlesome scribe who was a far less godly man than Paul. I think that professor is absolutely wrong. If we're honest, like Mother Teresa, every one of us faces "dark nights of the soul." Every one of us struggles with the sinful nature, which puts up walls that prevent us from following God's direction for our lives.

Keep in mind that both Paul and Mother Teresa, even for all their honesty about their internal struggles, found a way to break through those dark, tough days and thoughts. Both of them could echo the apostle's words: "I've tried everything and nothing helps. I'm at the end of my rope. Is there no one who can do anything for me? Isn't that the real question? The answer, thank God, is that Jesus Christ can and does" (Romans 7:24-25, THE MESSAGE).

Mother Teresa didn't give up her faith, or stop her ministry, because there were times in her life when she faced those three stubborn questions. But if someone as godly as her could face a want for answers, then be assured there will be days when the answers we long for won't come easy for us either. In the crucible of home life, the pat answers we repeated in Sunday school become refined by fire.

David Van Biema, in a *TIME* magazine article about Mother Teresa, wrote, "That absence [of God's presence in her life] seems to have started at almost precisely the time she began tending the poor and dying in Calcutta."[12] She was faced with death and disease every day, and how in the world could a loving God let *this* child die—and that one live? Why did one person prosper while another suffered?

Mother Teresa served every single day in the war zone that was Calcutta's ghettos. Every day for decades she saw the poor, the sick, and the dying. Every day she saw pictures that would be painful for anyone to see, even if they'd supposedly seen it all. And there would be pain. And with the pain, the questions would come. *Who is this God I am serving? What is really true about this upside-down world where I live? And why am I here in the first place?*

## THREE QUESTIONS . . . ONE TRUE ANSWER

The question Thomas asked revealed the tremendous testing he was experiencing. His three-tiered inquiry demonstrated the very same questions that come up in every test for all of us. But the Lord answered the complex question with a simple answer—and yet he answered every question more completely than anyone could have imagined: "I am the way, the truth, and the life" (John 14:6).

Amazingly, all three questions had the same response: "I am."

Several years ago, my family had the opportunity to travel to Rome, Italy, on vacation. The first day we were in the city, I made the executive decision that we should set out on our journey with only a map and our tennis shoes. After all, how hard could it be to navigate around one town?

*"I am the way, the truth, and the life."*
John 14:6

It may have been the most inefficient day in our traveling lives. We wandered up and down streets looking for the right ones. We searched far too long to find the right spot for lunch. We saw only a few of the key sights that were on our list and some that we couldn't even identify with our travel books. To make matters worse, my map was written (of all things) in *Italian*! (How thoughtless of them.)

We made it back to our hotel that evening utterly exhausted and looking very much like the tourists we were. Lana convinced me to talk with the concierge about reserving a tour guide for the next day, and I was glad to admit defeat.

When we entered the lobby on our second morning, it is hard to express how amazingly different things were. Giovana, an art history PhD, greeted us warmly and immediately hailed a taxi. She whisked us to our first stop in a matter of minutes and explained every fascinating detail of the sites even as we drove along. The entire day was exhilarating, like living a special on the Travel Channel! She took us to restaurants where only the locals dined and no English was spoken. She found ways to move ahead of the long lines into museums. She even showed us the best places to purchase souvenirs without getting ripped off.

About halfway through the day, as we were walking through the ruins of the ancient metropolis, it dawned on me that I had forgotten to bring my trusty map along for the journey. How could I have been so dependent on that map on one day, only to have it become an afterthought the next? Because one day I had a map, and the next day I had Giovana. I didn't need to know the way; she *was* the way.

The real secret to answering all three questions lies in Jesus. He carries us to the recipe for life-changing Faith Breakthroughs: the answer to every question is found in God himself. And every promise, every purpose, every worthwhile choice from this page forward will completely depend on our understanding Jesus' foundational answer.

"Lord, who is God?"

*"I am the way."*

"Lord, what is true?"

*"I am the truth."*

"Lord, why am I here?"

*"I am the life."*

Thomas's question shows the questions that times of testing often bring to mind. But Jesus' answer can tear down our walls and bring us both the direction and sense of perspective we need in an incredibly confusing world.

In Christ Jesus, we have everything we need to tear down the walls that are holding us back. He is the Giver of the promises. He offers the power to choose those promises. He provides the freedom to share those promises. And he strengthens us with the power to endure the testing of those promises—even the testing that comes through questions to which he is the one true answer.

## DISCUSSION QUESTIONS

1. "Who is God?" is a question we can never fully answer, though we may fall into the trap of thinking we have God completely figured out. Why is it a danger to assume we know everything there is to know about God?

2. Why is it so important to wrestle with the questions "Who is God?" and "What is True?" before trying to establish the purpose for our times of testing?

3. Mother Teresa wrestled with some tough questions about her faith and her God. If you were to write a letter to God that was as honest as Mother Teresa's, what questions would you ask him?

# *Brett & Kristen*
## WHEN WALLS BECOME BREAKTHROUGHS

*Brett grew up as* a nomad. By the time he was fifteen years old, his family had lived in twenty-three different places. In contrast, Kristen spent the first twenty-three years of her life in the same home. While their family backgrounds were different, their life story together is a beautiful example of a promise tested—and tested again.

Their story together began in high school, when he was eighteen and she was fifteen.

Brett joined the Navy right after high school, and he and Kristen stayed close during his seven years in the service. Halfway through his enlistment, Brett popped the question, Kristen said yes, and they were married, even though they would spend the next three years living apart. Kristen had just completed her nursing degree at UT Tyler when Brett was discharged from the Navy on the West Coast. He then enrolled at Texas A&M University, where he spent the next four and a half years completing engineering degrees while Kristen worked in the local emergency room. After being married for three years, they were finally together, life was good, and their plans began to take shape.

They soon became involved in a weekly Bible study. Brett had become a believer at fifteen and Kristen at age ten. Their faith grew as they met a great group of young couples, several of whom are still close friends today.

Both Brett and Kristen were smart and successful, and things were moving according to their script. After Brett finished engineering school, both quickly landed jobs in Austin, Kristen as a maternity-ward nurse and Brett as an engineer. Meaning double income. No kids. A house and all that went with it. But no worries. They had their lives mapped out, and those perks and responsibilities were part of it. They again got involved in an outstanding church and spent their time serving with others. Life was good and on-target.

That is, until Brett and Kristen decided it was time to start their family. That's when their plan got derailed. Weeks soon turned into months and then into years. Most couples they knew already had a child or two. While they had been certain they could easily join these budding young families when they chose, it became obvious that life wasn't taking shape as they had planned. What had gone wrong? They had planned everything out and done everything right, hadn't they?

If you've never dealt with infertility, it may not register how a dozen times a day you can trip over a reminder that you don't have a child. Every weekend it seems there's a birthday party for a friend's or a relative's child. There's Mother's Day at church, women with strollers everywhere at the mall, and movie portrayals of mothers with young children that give a Technicolor reminder of what's missing from your life. And for Kristen, there was the added reminder of working each day, caring for other people's newborns. Every day involved witnessing births, seeing the joy in those families' lives, and wondering, *Why not me, Lord? Why is life not going as planned?*

By now, several of their close couple friends were having their second child, if not their third. As their anxiety mounted and they became discouraged and disheartened, they experienced brokenness. But it was in their brokenness that their first wall began to shudder and then break as they turned to the Lord for help. The Psalms became their solitude, expression, and comfort through those difficult times. In the early days of doubt and hurt, and even as their wall began to crumble, they claimed the cry of David's broken heart as their own:

- The righteous cry, and the LORD hears and delivers them out of all their troubles. (Psalm 34:17, NASB)

- The LORD is near to the brokenhearted and saves those who are crushed in spirit. (Psalm 34:18, NASB)

But even as their Wall of Self-sufficiency was crumbling, other walls crept up to replace it. At different times they considered adoption. After three years of trying to conceive a child and more time dealing with fertility specialists, Brett's logical engineer's mind calculated well before Kristen that adoption needed to be an option in their plan. Kristen had been adopted, and it was clear to Brett that parents could love an adopted child as deeply as they could their own biological child. While Kristen certainly knew the same, she still felt a deep, aching desire to experience pregnancy, like she'd seen so many times in the lives of her friends, family, and patients.

Again, it was in the Lord that they both found resolution to this Wall of Confusion and eventually came to agree on adoption as a path. Miraculously, within months, God provided a beautiful daughter through an open adoption, meaning the birth mother was directly involved in meeting and selecting them, and Kristen was even inside the delivery room when their daughter was born.

Several years passed, including one heartbreaking failed adoption when the birth mother decided to parent her child herself when Brett and Kristen were twenty minutes from the hospital. Although it was well-intended, the resulting attention from concerned family and friends felt overwhelming, and another wall went up. Brett and Kristen withdrew into their lives of privacy once again, and their pursuit of adoption was shelved. Yet even while they were tremendously blessed and grateful for their daughter, Kristen still felt a tremendous ache and unfulfilled desire in her life.

Pregnancy was still a possible option. Kristen knew her biological clock was ticking, and visits to more fertility specialists revealed the need for more medically advanced options. Brett and Kristen found themselves facing yet another wall in their journey with infertility. Their previous experience had guided them to lean on the Lord, and God soon brought them their second child, a precious son, through another open adoption.

That child brought both of them something else as well: a chance to know God's Word promised, chosen, and tested as it broke down wall after wall of doubt, anxiety, unbelief, and longing. Brett recalls Psalm 9:10, the Scripture that spoke to him through this breakthrough: "Those who know your name trust in you, for you, O LORD, do not abandon those who search for you." For Kristen, it was Philippians 4:6-7, which asks God to deal with our hurt and anxiety, and promises us his peace beyond comprehension. Today, Kristen can honestly say that God has granted her a peace and joy in the blessings of her children through *his* plan, which is far beyond her missed experience of pregnancy.

I know that many reading this book can deeply relate to the steady, relentless, wall-raising ache that comes with an unfulfilled longing. Even when the longing is as pure and innocent as a couple who dreams of having a family of their own. And even in the presence of other very good things that God has placed in your life. Please know that breakthroughs can and do happen, just as they have for Brett and Kristen. In their brokenness they asked for God's help, and they saw their early Wall of Self-sufficiency come down. And even though they went on to face even bigger walls in their future, with God's help those walls would also fall and open their lives to an unexplainable, God-given sense of wholeness, peace, and rest. You can have the same kind of breakthrough in your life as well. (Find out more about Brett and Kristen's story at www.FaithBreakthroughs.com.)

# 3

# LIVING LIFE AS A
# WALL BREAKER

# chapter twelve

# DECLARING INDEPENDENCE FROM THE WALL

In the past eleven chapters, you've been given the raw materials to make a Faith Breakthrough. In these next four chapters, you'll be given four lessons in not just tearing down your wall, but moving past it to the exciting life beyond.

We'll talk in the next chapter about the most common fears that usually intrude on people who experience freedom after long periods of time behind a wall. You'll learn how to deal with obstacles like "breakdown friends," who are like people who put Krispy Kremes in your refrigerator when you're on a diet and all but recommend you go back behind your wall.

Before we're through, you will get some first steps to helping your children become wall breakers. You'll see the importance of both capturing your Faith Breakthrough story and then using it to help others. But living life as a wall breaker has to begin with a first step. My friend, it is time to take that step! As Daniel Henderson points out in his fantastic book *Fresh Encounters*, every believer must make a Declaration of Dependence upon God before real breakthroughs can take place. Beyond our dependence on God, however, we must also break loose of the barriers that the writer of Hebrews says can "so easily [trip] us up" (Hebrews 12:1). Only then will we know what it means to be free.

From the country of Abkhazia, whose citizens celebrate their independence from Georgia every September 30, to Zambia, where October 24 is their independence day from the United Kingdom, and for a very long list of countries in between, you can almost count on a country shutting down banks and government services and urging its people to participate in the celebration that marks a new beginning.

There's a lot to learn about life on the other side of the wall, but it begins with picking a day. On your calendar. Marked in red. And I'd suggest that it become a personal holiday, even if your celebration consists only of going home from work a few hours early or having a barbecue outside, even if you're going to be standing in snow while the hamburgers cook.

It's time to declare, in faith if your wall hasn't yet gone down, the truth of yet another promise of God:

> Therefore if anyone is in Christ, he is a new creature; the old things passed away; behold, new things have come. (2 Corinthians 5:17, NASB)

Ask almost any professional athletes what they're doing before a game or a match, and what will they tell you? Rehearsing the

As a matter of review, let's consider your journey so far.
I encourage you to take a few moments to reflect on and
then complete the following statements:

The primary wall or walls I am facing in my life:

_____

_____

_____

The promises that God has made me to overcome that wall:

_____

_____

_____

The steps I need to take to actively live those promises:

_____

_____

_____

The people with whom I have shared my wall—and my
path to the breakthrough:

_____

_____

_____

best ski run of their lives. Picturing themselves turning and deflecting the football just in time. Following through after the serve to be ready for the volley. Mentally going through what they've practiced time and again at the foul line.

There's a reason why it is important to "see" ourselves after the game and as having done well. And there's a reason why it's important to "see" who we are in Christ. As new creatures. The issue is not whether we've dropped the ball in the past, or left the wall up too long. What's important is that "new things have come." And to get ready for those first steps into freedom, it's important for each of us to say, "Today, on my independence day, and from this day forward, things have changed."

> *The issue is not whether we've dropped the ball in the past, or left the wall up too long. What's important is that "new things have come."*

Those of us who live in the United States celebrate our independence from Great Britain on July 4. If you ask the average person on the street when the Revolutionary War ended, many will say, "July 4th. I get off work that day every year!" Most of us have seen pictures of V-E Day and V-J Day (Victory in Europe Day and Victory in Japan Day) with sailors kissing nurses in Times Square, and some think that Independence Day was when the war ended and we were free.

But freedom didn't come to the new United Colonies on their "Independence Day." If you think back to American history class, you'll remember that we *declared* our independence from Britain on July 4, 1776, but the *war* for independence didn't end until October 19, 1781! Hostilities did not stop until General Charles Cornwallis, surrounded and pounded day and night for months with cannon and small-arms fire, surrendered the seven thousand British troops under his command. Not until that day were Americans free.

Can you see now why declaring an "Independence Day," even if you're still at the beginning or in the midst of your battle with a Wall of Doubt, or Worry, or Anger, is such an important thing to do?

*You simply must declare victory on this side of the wall.*

And it's important that you do it today, even if there's a fight ahead of you in discovering, choosing, and sharing a promise. When the fledgling American colonists declared their independence, a major change took place. From that day on, they looked at themselves differently. They were a new country, with a new name and a new future.

And keep one more thing in mind. Jesus spoke to the Pharisees who wanted to keep the status quo. They were furious with Jesus when he promoted new freedoms, like his disciples' eating grain on the Sabbath, or new capacities for growth and life, like when Jesus healed a hemorrhaging woman and a man born blind on the Sabbath.

As far as the Pharisees were concerned, nothing in Jesus' words or actions was true. It was the old that mattered, not the newness of life that Jesus showed in his miracles and would prove with his resurrection. Jesus told them people can't act like they're living in the old when all things have become new. He said:

No one sews a patch of unshrunk cloth on an old garment; otherwise the patch pulls away from it,

the new from the old, and a worse tear results. No
one puts new wine into old wineskins; otherwise the
wine will burst the skins, and the wine is lost and
the skins as well; but one puts new wine into fresh
wineskins. (Mark 2:21-22, NASB)

You can't live on both sides of the wall any more than you
can put old wine in new wineskins. The Pharisees could say
anything they wanted, but as one of the leaders of our country's independence, John Adams, once said, "facts are stubborn things." You can't put new wine in old wineskins. New
requires new, and if you're going to make a breakthrough, it's
time to declare, in faith, that you're moving forward. It's time
to think like—to believe like—someone who is beginning a
whole new adventure of faith.

If you have identified your wall and made a commitment
to break through, then it's time to write out your declaration.

> You can't live on
> both sides of the
> wall any more
> than you can put
> old wine in new
> wineskins.

It may seem like a silly practice, but do
not underestimate the power of making a
declaration. I encourage you to prayerfully
complete the following statement and to
share it with someone you love. Celebrate
it together! You're on your way to a breakthrough.

When you complete this declaration,
let me encourage you to do something
very unselfish that could make a huge difference in the life of someone facing the same wall you're
facing. Take a moment to log on to www.FaithBreakthroughs
.com and make your declaration public for others on the

same journey. Then, as you continue on the journey toward your Faith Breakthrough, you will do so along with those who have been inspired by people like you who led the way.

## DISCUSSION QUESTIONS

1. When you think of a "declaration of independence," what emotions are stirred within you?

2. Some people mistakenly think freedom means we can do whatever we want, but that mentality often leads us only into a new place of bondage—to a new set of walls. What is the difference between declaring absolute freedom and declaring independence from our walls?

3. Why is it important to declare independence even when you may still be fighting the battles?

4. What are some personal declarations you have made?

## MY DECLARATION OF INDEPENDENCE

May the Lord bless, keep, and guide me from this day forward. And may I walk in truth and life and the reality that on this, my independence day, my God has given me all I need to keep moving forward toward his best each day to come.

This day, _____, 20____, I declare as my independence day. The walls I face may be great, but my Lord is greater by far. In humility and faith I claim God's promise to me that "new things" have come (2 Corinthians 5:17, NASB). And though challenging days lie ahead, I know that God has already won the victory for me and that who I am and will be is different from who I was.

Signed this independence day by

_____

# chapter thirteen

# THOSE CHALLENGING FIRST STEPS TOWARD FREEDOM

Life on the other side of the wall is filled with freedom and energy and direction and purpose and hope. It's also rife with scary moments as we take those first steps. Ask a prisoner finally set free. Ask an addict about the challenges of life after sobriety. The moments after walls come down can be exhilarating, but reality sets in that those same walls can be built again very quickly if the promises are forgotten.

Once when Jesus walked on the water to catch up to his disciples in a boat, Peter boldly asked whether he could walk on water as well (Matthew 14:22-33). Jesus invited him to come out, and Peter counted on Christ's promise that it could be done. Peter is the only man in history who trusted God enough to walk on water! But soon the waves became increasingly rough, and Peter got nervous. He took his eyes off Jesus and began sinking.

In a matter of moments, he had gone from a man of great faith to a man with rapidly sinking optimism. Of course, Jesus reached out his hand and rescued Peter, but not before we were all reminded just how frail our faith can be.

In our walk with Lily, and in facing the walls that accompanied the challenges we have faced, we know well how quickly walls can be reconstructed during the storms of life—especially when life takes a second downward turn after progress has been made.

After the first year of heart surgery, intestinal complications, and breathing episodes, we had every reason to believe that Lily's health was turning around, that smooth sailing would now chart the course for a happily-ever-after ending. And for the months following her birthday, that seemed to be just the case. We enjoyed reading books together, playing peekaboo, finding noses, and all of the other simple things that normally accompany toddler life.

However, just before family vacation, Lana and I began to admit what we were seeing take place. Subtly, Lily's words began to disappear. She disconnected from others and began to shrink into her own little world. We watched the regression with a panic that we would have felt regardless of her past but that seemed to be an even lower blow considering how far we'd come.

More testing and doctor visits ensued. Different theories and diagnoses came. Perhaps this was a reaction to the bypass surgery, which some studies indicated was not uncommon. Maybe her hearing was to blame. Others believed the combination of her immunizations and her frail weight due to the heart issues had led to autism. The only thing that mattered, however, was that Lily was going backward and there was nothing we could do about it. Lily began a rigorous program of therapies, and we began researching ravenously in search of the right solution.

That pursuit has continued to this day and has led to many new disappointments. It has also kept the walls in our peripheral vision, an ever-present danger as we walk through the battles. A few months ago, Lily was brought in to a special program for kids who cannot speak. It seemed to Lana and me that this was the perfect match we'd been waiting for, the beginning of the story of her recovery. But there was one catch—the school wisely required that the children experience a three-day trial period before they were offered enrollment.

We prayerfully dropped Lily off the first day and waited to hear from the school. Lana called me that afternoon and said things had gone very well. At last, there was hope! The second day we dropped her off together and even went for coffee to celebrate how things were going. I went off to work and came home to hear the next good report.

Unfortunately, the good report never came. When Lana stopped crying enough to tell me what had happened, she shared that the directors of the school were not convinced that Lily would thrive in their system. Because of her inability to respond to simple commands, she could not be enrolled. The staff at that wonderful school were doing what they felt was best for our daughter, and they were not to blame. But our hopes had been raised to a level we hadn't experienced in months, and then they were shattered.

We held each other and cried. All of the pain and disappointment, the fear of the future, and the despair of not knowing what should happen next left us feeling stuck all over again. In the midst of that pain, God prompted my spirit in a way that I will never forget. I was drawn back to all of the promises we had clung to in the midst of the heart surgery, the same promises that seemed so far away in the face of our bad news.

I looked at Lana and said, "You know, I feel like God is telling me that if I really believe that walls can come down—if I really believe that he offers the power of the breakthrough, then right now is the time to stand on that power. Let's stop and think about the promises he has for us."

We took the next few minutes to share again the promises that had grown to mean so much. They were different for each of us. Lana's wall was primarily one of doubt—doubt that God was able to heal our daughter, and confusion as to why he would choose not to. She shared again how she was clinging to promises like Psalm 126:3, 5-6: "Yes, the LORD has done amazing things for us! What joy! . . . Those who plant in tears will harvest with shouts of joy. They weep as they go to plant their seed, but they sing as they return with the harvest."

My wall was primarily a Wall of Fear that the worst could happen in my daughter's life, and I would have no way to prevent it. I reminded her of the promises I had held close in recent months—promises like Philippians 4:6-7: "Don't worry about anything; instead, pray about everything. Tell God what you need, and thank him for all he has done. Then you will experience God's peace, which exceeds anything we can understand. His peace will guard your hearts and minds as you live in Christ Jesus."

As we remembered our walls and shared the promises that had been so powerful in helping us through them, hope began to reappear. I'd be lying if I told you that everything became happy and joyful in the room that day. But without the reminder of those promises, I think we'd have sunk into the waves just like Peter. And I'm honestly not sure I could have completed this book.

Never take the promises you have received for granted. Dwell on them often. In the Rush family, every day brings with it a new decision of whether to dwell on the promises or the circumstances. This book is full of real-life stories that share happy endings, but that's not always the way life goes. Our breakthroughs are far more than checking off items on a list. And we have to face the fact that our walls are always one unhealthy mind-set away. We are one diagnosis, or one bit of bad news, away from forgetting the good news from the past.

> *Never take the promises you have received for granted. Dwell on them often.*

It is imperative that you prepare for those moments before they happen. Place symbols and reminders in your home. Tell your friends and family so that they can constantly remind you as well. Don't ever settle for life behind the wall again.

## THE ENEMY'S ROLE AFTER THE BREAKTHROUGH

It's not just our fear of what people will think or say or how they will react that can worry us when a wall goes down and we're ready to step forward toward God and others. There's something else we must keep in mind as well.

The enemy of the breakthrough, Satan himself, doesn't appreciate when walls are flattened. He's more than willing to paint a beautiful memory of life as it was before the wall, no matter how much of a trash heap the old life might have been. The enemy doesn't value freedom and life and love and forgiveness. Even though God's promises opened up the big hole we've walked through, there will always be those times when we can give in and say, "Maybe I should go back. Maybe it wasn't so bad when the wall was up. This is too hard. Too unfamiliar."

> *Satan will paint a beautiful memory of life as it was before the wall, no matter how much of a trash heap the old life might have been.*

In my experiences leading others toward Faith Breakthroughs, and living my own, I have found that Satan uses three primary weapons to keep us from enjoying life beyond the walls. All three can creep in subtly without our even being aware of a problem, and all three can be overcome as long as we are watching for the dangers.

### The first weapon of the enemy: unsupportive friends

Your first glance at that heading might have been confusing. How on earth could our friends and family keep us from a breakthrough? Aren't they part of the solution? And the answer should be yes: friends and family should be a very important part of this whole journey. But surrounding yourself with people who don't really comprehend the power of Faith Breakthroughs can also make it very difficult to get beyond and remain past your walls.

Watch out for friends whose bad habits lead you away from God's promises. I like to call them "breakdown friends," because that is what they often unwittingly help you accomplish.

Remember how Job had a group of friends who really didn't seem like such good friends? (Some of them just told him he was the problem and to lie down and die. That's not great to hear from a friend!) As you take those first steps through and past your spiritual walls, you absolutely, positively need to have a group of companions to help you move toward God's best.

I highly encourage you to look around at those who are influencing you the most right now. If they are breakdown friends instead of wall breakers, now's the time to kindly and prayerfully start moving toward new peers who can help you move forward, not back.

God's Word says, "Bad company corrupts good character" (1 Corinthians 15:33). Bad company can also weaken your resolve to move forward, or start you thinking about heading back behind an old wall. Take a look at these characteristics of breakdown friends, and see if any of these influences are active in your life.

**Breakdown friends can never admit a fault.** There is something about humility and admitting we're wrong that helps tear down walls. You have to come to a place of acknowledging the lies that are holding you back before you can recognize where God's promises need to be addressed in your life. That level of honest authenticity often brings discomfort.

Proverbs 9:8 shares this principle in a way we can all relate to: "Don't bother correcting mockers; they will only hate you. But correct the wise, and they will love you."

People who never admit a fault or failure can wear on us, and they can wear off on us as well. Pray to lay down your pride as you seek to break down walls, and take a time-out from friends who see admitting any weakness as a sign of weakness. Instead, pray about and look for people who aren't too cool to say, "I'm sorry" without sarcasm, or, "What can I do to make that right?" instead of "I'm always right." Positive wall-breaker friends have a humility about them because they already know they aren't, and don't have to be, perfect! Look for grace-based friends like that.

**Breakdown friends look for ways around God's Word.** Of course, the tendency to twist or rationalize the truth of God's Word started when Satan tempted Eve with his question, "Did God really say you must not eat the fruit from any of the trees in the garden?" (Genesis 3:1). We can see the same strategy in his temptation of Christ: "If you are the Son of God, tell these stones to become loaves of bread" (Matthew 4:3). Certainly, Satan was no "friend" to Eve or Jesus, and that fallen angel's trickery isn't good to have in our closest circle of friends either.

Breakdown friends look for creative ways around God's Word. They try to move you an inch away from your resolve to trust God and focus on his promises, much like someone saying to you when you're trying so hard on a diet, "Oh, it's just *one* cookie." And unfortunately, their encouragement to cut corners can influence you to stumble in your commitment. If your friends encourage you to "forget" what's legal or right, they can cause you to take one little step, then another, until you're back behind your wall instead of breaking through it.

Look for and seek out friends who look for ways to keep God's Word, friends who join with you in trusting and choosing his promises, not questioning and nibbling away at what you know God is asking you to do.

**Breakdown friends focus on image rather than honesty.** There's a third kind of person who can make it very challenging when you're working toward a Faith Breakthrough. That's someone who does good things for the wrong reason—to be seen as good.

Here's an example. I recently heard a friend describe his difficult childhood and the pain of having a father who was seldom there. His dad rarely came home at night, and he eventually left home for good. He wasn't there for his wife or children most of the week, but he would make sure he was always at home on Sunday afternoon. Why? Because they lived in a town where many parents took their kids in strollers or on bikes along a long beltway path, and families would meet and stop and talk. And this man wanted to look like a family man on those Sunday walks because that's when he'd strike up conversations that were actually "leads" for calls to sell insurance during the week!

If the dad in that story reminds you of someone close to you, you certainly need to pray for him or her. However, you also need to back away from spending all your time with this person. Remember this: when you put a white glove in the mud, the mud doesn't become "glovey." The glove becomes muddy. King Saul in the Bible was that kind of image manager, someone who cared more about being seen with the prophet Samuel in public than about doing what was right before God in private.

As a pastor, I've seen the tragedy of families deciding it was easier to put on masks than to cry out for the help they really needed. There will always be the temptation, and sadly the encouragement from some well-meaning friends or family, to just sweep issues under the rug, to cover up problems, to pretend that a wall doesn't exist, or to simply pretend that it's just an unavoidable part of life.

Surround yourself with people who are authentic enough to be who they really are, who seek truth even when that means exposing the challenges and walls of life.

I don't want to discourage you if you've got one of each of those breakdown friends in your speed dial! Remember, no one is perfect, and the answer to tearing down walls isn't to walk or run away from people. But it's important to remember that God's Word is true. "Bad company corrupts good character." Seek out the kind of friends that are wall breakers and minimize the influence of any breakdown friends.

In fact, as you move forward, you'll become one of those wall-breaker friends yourself, challenging those around you to move toward God's best.

### The second weapon of the enemy: unsubstantiated fears

It took only a split second on that cool August night in Montreal's Olympic Stadium for it to happen. Standing sixty and a half feet straight out from home plate, Dave Dravecky's future as a Major League baseball pitcher ended in the midst of a pitch. In the instant it took for his arm to snap, all his carefully laid plans were shattered. With a sickening *crack*, his dreams of a comeback ended. All the time he had spent battling back from having cancer removed from his left arm, all the rehab he'd done, came to nothing. His Cinderella story ended like a nightmare.

In the weeks that followed, the decisions were agonizing, the prayers real, and the surgery radical. The doctors shared the somber news that Dave's arm was shattered beyond repair and would have to be amputated. And part of his shoulder as well.

As Dave shared in his powerful autobiography, *Comeback*, the promises of God sustained him in ways he could have never imagined. God remained with him, and provided a peace that defies all human understanding. In the midst of some of the most rigorous tests and trials one could imagine, the Lord was faithful. Dave Dravecky knew full well what it meant to experience a Faith Breakthrough.

Still, after the surgery came and went, there were many difficult first steps to take. Like the first time Dave forced himself to stand in front of the mirror and look at the hole where his arm had been, or his first time of struggling to get a shirt buttoned with one hand. There was the first time he stared at his shoelaces and wondered how in the world he was going to tie them and the first time he experienced the phantom pain that felt as if his fingertips were on fire, even though there were no fingers to feel anything.

But none of those were the most fearful first steps for Dave. Even though the walls of unhealthy mind-sets were coming down because of his faith, there remained a step that scared him to death: the daunting task of facing his children for the first time, not knowing how they would respond to a dad who was suddenly missing an arm.

Dave and Jan had decided not to have the kids come to the hospital during his short stay there after the amputation. Instead, the day Dave came home, they brought each child into the room, one at a time, to see Daddy.

Their son, Jonathan, was the first to come in. An energetic nine-year-old at the time, he loved baseball and his father. He walked into the room and then slowly walked around, looking at his father from all angles, without saying anything.

Finally, Dave broke the silence and asked Jonathan, "Well, do you want to see my scar?"

"Yeah!" Jonathan said, his eyes lighting up.

Carefully, Dave had his son help him remove the massive bandages that covered the site of his amputation, and Dave told his son what the surgeons had done and how well the doctors thought the surgery had gone.

Far from being upset or grossed out, his son said, "Wow, Dad! Wait right here! Don't move a muscle. I'll be right back, I promise. Don't go anywhere!"

Dave didn't go anywhere, and sure enough, very shortly Jonathan came back in the room and said, "Dad, I've got some of my friends outside. Can they come in and see your scar, too?"

Any fears that Dave might have had about his son being distant or uncomfortable around him were dispelled in those moments. But then the most fearful moment of all awaited him.

How would his daughter, Tiffany, feel when she saw her daddy without an arm? Would an empty sleeve put a barrier between the two of them?

It turned out that their daughter had been outside the room the whole time, waiting patiently for her turn to come in. When Jan told her she could go see her father, she ran inside the room and right over to her father. And when she reached him, he did something he hadn't been able to do for a number of weeks before his surgery because of the pain in his arm—he was able to give his daughter a big hug with his strong right arm.

They held each other for a long time, and then as Tiffany sat in his lap, he looked at his daughter and asked, hopefully, "Well, what do you think?"

"Daddy," she said, "I'm glad they took your arm off."

"You are?" he asked, taken off guard. "Why?"

"I'm glad they took your arm off because you can hug me again."

Did you notice that the fears that had overwhelmed him the most were completely unfounded? By God's grace, his children had already been prepared to love their father unconditionally. But fear can overwhelm all of us. Neale Donald Walsch has said that FEAR is an acronym for "False Evidence Appearing Real."

As traumatic as his experience was, Dave Dravecky wasn't broken by what happened to him. Shaken? Yes. Set back from the life he'd planned? Absolutely. But in Christ, he had absolutely nothing to fear.

### The third weapon of the enemy: undeserved fondness
Historian Stephanie Coontz wrote a book a few years ago titled *The Way We Never Were*. In it she shared evidence that many have made "the good old days" out to be something

far more pleasant than what was actually true. We all have a tendency to conveniently remember only the good parts of the past, almost as if our minds have put away the bad stuff as a defense mechanism. That's probably a good thing, but it can become a danger when we convince ourselves that life behind the wall was somehow glorious and pain-free.

*The Shawshank Redemption* is an Academy Award–winning movie that gives an unforgettable and brutal picture of life behind prison walls. It's a gripping story of friendship and suffering and of what one man risks for freedom. But while its message is redeeming, one of the saddest parts of the movie is what happens to Brooks Hatlen, one of the inmates you grow to care for.

Brooks is the librarian at Shawshank State Prison. He's an old-timer who has spent all of his adult life behind bars. But then an unexpected (and, for Brooks, unwanted) surprise results in his finally being paroled. He walks through the walls that have defined him for so long into a virtual unknown. So much has changed since he went to prison. He is given a job on the outside in a grocery store and the key to a small room in a halfway house that accepts ex-cons. But he's spent so many years behind bars that his life falls apart.

Earlier in the film, the character Red (played by Morgan Freeman), who is the main narrator of the story, says something that becomes a dramatic theme as the movie and time progresses.

"These walls are funny," Red says. "First you hate 'em, then you get used to 'em. Enough time passes, you get so you depend on them."

As bad as it was behind those walls (and in the movie it's

terribly bad for the inmates), spending enough time behind walls leaves Brooks unprepared for life on the other side.

"I have trouble sleepin' at night," he confesses in a letter to "the fellas" who were his friends and messmates in the prison. As they read Brooks's letter, the viewer sees Brooks shuffling from his job at the grocery to his small room, trying to deal with all the new changes and fearful of the freedom that gives him so much time to be alone (something he didn't have in prison). Brooks shares poignantly in a letter to his friend Andy Dufresne, "I have bad dreams like I'm falling. I wake up scared. Sometimes it takes me a while to remember where I am. Maybe I should get me a gun, and rob the Foodway so they'd send me home."

But he's too old and broken by life to do that. And after writing his letter, he steps off a chair and hangs himself.

It's not just in a movie script but also in Scripture that you see people who are fearful and struggle with coming out from behind walls. That's what happened to the nation of Israel after their years of slavery in Egypt.

If you're not familiar with the story, God's people had been in captivity for *four hundred years*. Then almighty God raised up Moses, his servant, who dramatically led the people out of Egypt and got them on the road to the Promised Land. But no sooner had they left Egypt than Pharaoh had a change (or hardening) of heart. He decided they shouldn't be free and raced out after God's people with his horde of war chariots.

It looked like God's people would be decimated, as they had run out of room to escape and were backed up right against the Red Sea. But I hope you've at least seen the movie, if not read it in Scripture, and know how almighty God had

Moses lift his staff above his head. When Moses did, the waters of the sea parted, and God's people were saved! But not the Egyptians who were foolish enough to follow.

You would think after that kind of dramatic rescue God's people would think this freedom thing was incredible! After all, they were headed in a positive direction toward a new land God promised was flowing with milk and honey. They had seen their God fight for them and had seen what no person on earth had ever seen before—walls of water standing up so that they could flee from their walls of slavery.

But then the second-guessing started—and it might happen for you as well. After the excitement wore off from leaving behind their walls, there came a time of testing and trial. For these people, it was when they ran out of water. You'd think they just might trust that if God could deliver them through water, he could provide water. But instead they grumbled and complained, sounding just like Red with his walls.

"First you hate 'em, then you get used to 'em. Enough time passes, you get so you depend on them."

They cried out in frustration, not faith:

Why did you bring us out here to die in the wilderness? Weren't there enough graves for us in Egypt? What have you done to us? Why did you make us leave Egypt? Didn't we tell you this would happen while we were still in Egypt? We said, "Leave us alone! Let us be slaves to the Egyptians. It's better to be a slave in Egypt than a corpse in the wilderness!" (Exodus 14:11-12)

When we face trials, even after we've discovered, chosen, and shared a promise—even after we've been through the fire of testing as well—we too can believe life was better behind the wall. Emotions may deceive us, but we must never forget that life wasn't better behind the wall. And it's never God's will or plan for us to accommodate barriers of unhealthy mind-sets in our life.

For many of us, a wall going down doesn't automatically mean we know how to move forward toward God's best, or even how to move toward others who may have broken down the same kind of wall. Many of us can remember amazing news pictures of the day the Berlin Wall came down. But in reality, it took months and years for the two nations to reunite, and those on both sides had to take fearful first steps.

> *It's never God's will or plan for us to accommodate barriers of unhealthy mind-sets in our life.*

## THE THREE QUESTIONS AND LIFE AFTER THE WALL

For each of us, circumstances—especially negative ones—can lead to either breakdowns or breakthroughs. Dave Dravecky had every opportunity to proclaim that God had forgotten him. And just like the Berlin Wall was really a series of walls, Dave had to face some new challenges after he finally moved past the first one. He could have asked the three test questions we discussed in chapter 11 and walked away disappointed. He instead chose to stand on what he knew to be true regardless of the circumstances.

Do you see how these questions can make the walls seem so daunting, and make moving on so difficult? Dave Dravecky and his wife no doubt were faced with asking, "Who is God? Can he hear our prayers? And why didn't he do what we asked?"

These questions led to asking, "What is true? If God is who he says he is, then why would such a thing happen to such a good person?"

And finally, the question "Why am I here?" created the danger of falling behind another Wall of Inadequacy, or Fear, or Shame, in facing his children.

Dave's story led to a Faith Breakthrough, but perhaps now you see why I started this book by saying it's not such a simple process. It might be difficult for him to tell you where one breakthrough was accomplished and a new wall was faced. Difficult circumstances are not walls, but challenges such as these can often lead to multiple walls that must be faced with multiple promises.

Whether it's the fear that comes with not knowing how others will react to our new commitments and direction, like Dave Dravecky with his children, or a released prisoner, or the nation of Israel, the temptation to move backward must be addressed daily. Never forget the promises that have brought you this far.

## DISCUSSION QUESTIONS

1. Even when we remember all of the problems that came with the walls in our lives, why do you think it is still so tempting to fall back into that place of unbelief?

2. You will not be able to avoid some unhelpful friends and family members in the midst of your breakthrough. What are some practical ways of protecting yourself from their negative influences?

3. Think of some of the greatest fears people face, or if you're honest enough, think of some of your own. Ask yourself, "What is the absolute worst thing that can happen?" Then ask, "Would that outcome keep God from loving me or keep me from his presence?" If you are fearful about a current situation, you might even ask, "What are the best things that can happen out of the present circumstances?"

# chapter fourteen

# RAISING WALL BREAKERS IN YOUR HOME

It may be hard for an egg to turn into a bird:
it would be a jolly sight harder for it to learn to fly while
remaining an egg. We are like eggs at present. And you
cannot go on indefinitely being just an ordinary,
decent egg. We must be hatched or go bad.[13]

One day your kids and my kids, and others' kids in whose lives we may have some influence, will "hatch" into adults. As cute as they are when they're young, they stay young such a short time. So the question now is, what mark will we leave in their lives? What will we do now so that when they do hatch and fly away on their own, they will be in love with their Savior and know how to love others, wherever they land?

I love Aimee Bender's memories of walking through an antique store. She writes in her short story "Tiger Mending," "That's the thing about handmade items. They still have the person's mark on them, and when you hold them, you feel less alone."

It may seem far off, but the day is coming when, to our

children, we will have grown old, no matter how young we feel inside. And in those days when our direct influence has passed, we will have nevertheless left indelible marks that will remain for the rest of their lives—the kind of marks that people leave when they're making a handcrafted article. The kind of marks that will show if we were careful or hurried, kind or cruel. The kind of marks that will reveal whether our children stepped out on their own feeling alone or carrying the marks of our love upon them.

## THOSE HOLES IN MY HOMEWORK

I can remember in high school turning in paper after paper to my history teacher, Mr. Tortorette. I also got paper after paper back from Mr. Tortorette with a "signature" mark on each one. I don't mean a letter grade or scribbled corrections or comments written into the margins. I mean there was a mark (often several marks) on every paper I got back. They were small holes surrounded by light-brown stains, smoke holes from the cigarettes he must have chain-smoked as he was grading papers at night. I could just imagine him poring over our essays, cigarette perched between his lips, ashes escaping to the assignments below.

Over the years, I've often thought about those marks he left. Mr. Tortorette was passionate about the study of history, and he taught me a lot that year. But he also left those unintentional marks with me that he never even realized he was making, or never really cared about.

Still, the marks were there for all to see.

The marks of a mom or dad may be easier to hide, but

they are far more significant, dropped upon the lives of our children whether we intend to or not. That legacy will have an incredible impact on who our kids become. Our influence can work for good or ill, but it will be deeply embedded on the next generation as though burned on the pages of their hearts.

What marks will you leave on your child's life?

For Marian Wright Edelman, here are the marks her father left her:

I was fourteen years old the night my Daddy died. He had holes in his shoes . . . and a vision he was able to convey to me as he lay dying in an ambulance that I, a young Black girl, could be and do anything; that race and gender are shadows; and that character, self-discipline, determination, and attitude are the substance of life.[14]

Wow! I certainly don't want to lose my life when my daughters are young, but I long to leave that kind of mark on their lives. That's the first key thing to consider in raising a wall breaker. Our actions leave marks, good or bad.

*Our actions leave marks, good or bad.*

## OUR CHILDREN AS WHITEBOARDS

It's also important for us to understand that children want their parents to leave marks on their lives—at least of the good variety. Our children are like whiteboards longing for us to write things they can circle later, to which they can keep referring time and again. It may be a touch or a smile. It might be words like, "I'm proud of you!" or, "I love you so much," or, "You are such an answer to prayer." It could be a memory we write for them as we take a walk in the woods while thousands of leaves fall, or those marks that still remain from that one fishing trip full of mosquitoes and memories that still bring a smile. Every child wants to be marked by a home where he or she is loved and accepted. *Every one.*

Maya Angelou, in writing about the last episode of the television show *Cheers*, captures this idea: "The ache for home lives in all of us," she writes. "We ache for the safe place where we can go as we are and not be questioned."

That television show resonated with so many people, I believe, because it gave people a sense of place—a sense of home—that so many lack in our culture today. That sense of belonging was really designed by God to take place primarily in one location: the home. Few would argue that home life is in serious trouble in much of our culture, but I don't believe it will ever turn around until the walls of unhealthy mind-sets that have been built are torn down.

We can be the generation that breaks through the walls that are eroding all we hold dear. Walls of Resentment, Anger, Lust, and Greed—some of which were passed down by our own parents—are ready to be destroyed with the promises of God.

As we commit to this paramount challenge, we will raise a whole new generation of wall breakers. This commitment extends beyond only parents of young children. Every one of us who has the capacity and opportunity to impact the life of a child is a part of this high calling. And that opportunity is not only for moms and dads: regardless of your season of life, your experience and influence can make the difference for someone else's future.

## PING-PONG BALLS AND TEACHABLE MOMENTS

Living in a small Texas town during my high school years didn't always lead to the most exhilarating lifestyle. And as anyone who knows small-town life can tell you, when something unusual does take place, it captures a lot of attention. During the town's annual parade, the chamber of commerce came up with the idea that they would have my dad drop several thousand Ping-Pong balls from an airplane. This was to happen over the town square right after the festivities concluded on the ground. The intrigue heightened with the revelation that *one* Ping-Pong ball out of all of them would be specially marked, and whoever found it would win one thousand dollars!

The publicity stunt worked amazingly well. The local paper covered it for weeks leading up to the big day, and thousands gathered for the parade—the biggest crowd the town had ever seen. People covered the sidewalks just waiting for their chance to catch the marked ball when it was dropped. Unfortunately, as is often the case, things didn't go exactly as planned.

The wind that morning was gusting down at ground level and was even stronger as the plane approached the drop site. The people bustled about chaotically, not really certain what location was best, but not content to stand still.

After two passes, and a futile attempt to guess at what the wind patterns would do once the balls dropped, the balls began pouring out of the plane by the hundreds. What happened next can hardly be put into words. The small spheres began falling the thousand or so feet to the ground like tiny plastic snowflakes. The flight pattern seemed to be different for every ball, and they seemed to spread apart faster than they fell from the sky. You could see people running in all directions!

A sea of small objects would blow one way, and the masses would follow. They would blow another way, and others would turn in pursuit.

Believe it or not, no one ever found the ball with the special mark. I think they ended up having a drawing to give the money away. (If you're ever in Lockhart, Texas, keep an eye out for a marked Ping-Pong ball—you might still be the lucky winner!) Regardless, I was left with an unforgettable picture in my mind that speaks to me so much about my children at the stages of life they're in.

There is a time in our children's lives when they look up to us with excitement like those people looking up at the plane. They are excited to follow us, to be with us, to learn from us. They eagerly anticipate that those Ping-Pong balls we drop out of the plane will provide the treasure they so desperately need.

But it doesn't take long for children to grow up and to start chasing after other things. While their love for us and their need for our love doesn't change, they don't look up to us in the same way they once did. As a parent, you'll know it when that Ping-Pong ball season comes to an end, replaced by a desire for a more side-by-side relationship that can grow deeper and stronger, but different.

If you're slightly past that Ping-Pong ball point, don't give up the hope of getting through to your children. Just craft your sharing and teaching in a time frame and a manner that makes sense to who they are now. Remember, even when they don't act interested, there is always that ache and longing for a parent's involvement and investment in their lives. On the other hand, if you have very young children, then know that Ping-Pong ball season is coming, when their ears are most open. If that's the season you're enjoying today, don't take it for granted! It is a wonderful and unique time to be a parent. Finally, if that Ping-Pong ball season is long since over, then look for different ways of connecting and sharing and teaching.

Whatever the season, start now. Start realizing today that your children need to know about your love, and God's love, and how God's Word and promises can help them move toward his best for them. And what do you teach them?

We've done a lot of work at our church to help parents. And even beyond our church, helping people live out God's promises at home has been my passion for two decades. I have had the privilege of sharing the natural breakthrough process with churches around the world. Lord willing, I would love to share far more in a future book about the all-important opportunity we have to minister to children. In the meantime, keep tabs on www.FaithBreakthroughs.com and look for ongoing ideas just for parents and others who influence the lives of children.

None of us would argue that parenting is unimportant,

but few would likewise say that it is easy. I want to share several foundational truths I believe to be most critical.

## FOUR FUNDAMENTALS FOR RAISING WALL BREAKERS

1. **Teach them you love them.** My friend Dr. John Trent calls it "the blessing." My church has had the privilege of hosting Dr. Gary Chapman, and he says to wrap up what you want children to understand in their "love language." Whatever you call it, however you do it, job one in teaching children to become wall breakers is to show them your love, which will make it so much easier for them to see God's love for them in the days to come.

> *Teach children to become wall breakers by showing them your love, which will make it easier for them to see God's love for them.*

Remembering that we have only a season to reach our children should make us very aware of the messages we are sending every day—even the ones we don't mean to send.

Years ago, when I was leading a youth retreat for a church, I asked each student to draw a "family portrait," a simple picture that would best describe their home lives. One young lady drew a picture of a television, and that's all. She said, "All my father does is watch TV. We never talk." Another young man drew a huge canyon, with half of his family on one side and half on the other, explaining that there were always battles that separated them, and the children were always challenged to choose sides. I have held on to those drawings all these years because I never want to forget the impact of the little things on these teens and how critical my own actions are in the lives of my children. It is not only the words we say that make the impact, although words are important. Our children and teens are watching to see whether the God of the promises is really guiding us or if we are all talk.

Maybe you can relate to the "portraits" those students drew of their family lives, and perhaps you've experienced challenges like these yourself. But that doesn't mean you have to extend that legacy to the next generation. Maybe one of those kids is living in the house next door and you can be the vessel of God's blessing and promise that he or she so desperately needs.

To raise children who will one day be wall breakers, start off by helping them—in both word and deed—to know how loved, how special, and how important they are to you. Your words and actions will make it so much easier for them to see such a love that's always been there from their heavenly Father.

2. **Teach them that grace lives at home.** Grace has been defined by many theologians as "our riches at Christ's expense." While that is absolutely true, I like the literal meaning behind the word, which is "unmerited favor." Either way, we are given something (our riches) that we don't deserve (at Christ's expense).

Don't get me wrong. We provide the soft side and the hard side of love when it's needed for our children. We discipline them. We hold family meetings. We have attitude-adjustment walks and talks when needed, and we help our children set goals and send them to bed on time so they get enough sleep to be able to meet those goals. We're involved in their schools and love helping coach their teams and going with them on vacations. But there will come a time in each child's life when what he or she needs the most is just to know that we care—in spite of a broken marriage, or flunking out of a school, or dropping the pass that would have won a championship, or ending up like my friend did in the backseat of a squad car.

I mentioned Dr. John Trent earlier in the chapter. Many of us know him as a prolific author and speaker. What many may not know is that he grew up in a single-parent home. What he never had in a father, however, was more than made up for in his mother. Then, when John was in junior high and high school, rheumatoid arthritis dealt a devastating blow to his mom. She suffered more and more pain, went through more and more surgeries, and within two years was forced to retire from a job she loved. And she had to take so much pain medicine that she went to bed early, which made it all that much easier for her son to sneak out of the house to join up with some other boys making very poor choices. One night after he had sneaked out, John got picked up by the police at two o'clock in the morning.

Thankfully, the policeman took John to his home instead of to the juvenile detention center. But of course, that meant waking up John's mother and telling her what he'd done.

John had escaped one punishment, but he knew there was more to come. His mother pointed for him to sit at the kitchen table, and for the longest time she didn't say anything. Not a word. And as long seconds turned into minutes, John could see the hurt and pain he'd caused her by his behavior, added to the grinding pain from the arthritis that was ravaging her joints.

Finally, he couldn't take it anymore and blurted out, "Well, I guess this means you don't love me anymore."

His mother's head snapped up, and her slate gray eyes met his. "This has *nothing* to do with love," she told him. "I will *always* love you. But I am extremely disappointed in you."

John shared with me that he knew two things right then. First, that he was going to be grounded for a long time. But second, that no matter what—even if he was brought home by the police at two in the morning—his mother would love him. Unmerited favor. Undeserved love.

In the absence of her son's father, John Trent's mom reflected the unforgettable grace—and occasional tough love—of the heavenly Father. God's grace rang true for him, for he'd felt it in his heart of hearts first through his mother's love.

Helping our children know we love them is the first thing we can do to build wall breakers in our home. Extending grace is a second. Now let's look at a third that should be something we know a lot more about since we're this far along in the book!

3. **Teach them that spiritual walls need to come down.**
Several years ago, when we were living in another house,
I got a panicked call from Lana to come right home. As
soon as I arrived and looked around, I was sure she was
right. We had rats in our attic! What a terrible thought!
It felt like all of us, including the dogs, were suddenly
under attack by diseased vermin. Rats have been blamed
for spreading the plague, and now they were loose in our
attic.

We grabbed a phone book and called one of those
24-7 rat exterminators with the really big ads, and I
didn't even mind paying an extra service charge and
a time-and-a-half charge as well. After all, what price
could we put on keeping our family safe from the
plague?

Bravely the exterminator crawled into the attic, and
after a long time of looking, he finally came back down.

"You do not have rats," he said with finality.

We looked at him in confusion because something
was certainly running across the ceiling in several
rooms.

"You do not have rats. You have squirrels."

You can't imagine the relief that Lana and I felt.
The children were safe. The dogs were safe. I was safe
from having to battle any rats that might creep down
at night to attack the kids or the dogs. We had squirrels! Cute, cuddly—and that's when it hit us—*rodents*.
Squirrels are really just cute rats!

I share that story because it matters so much
what we call something. It matters how we look at

something. How we look at a problem makes a difference in how serious we are about dealing with it. With our children, it matters that we teach them never to settle for something less than God's best, no matter how comfortable that choice has become. Walls may seem cute like squirrels, but they're still rodents that need to go away.

The youth and children's ministries at Bannockburn are completely focused on challenging parents to take on the walls they are facing in their homes, even when it's uncomfortable. Carla Dillard, our children's minister, constantly challenges parents to live out God's promises before their children. She has created a culture among our moms and dads that sees an urgency to the breakthroughs every family so desperately needs, and that approach has paid incredible dividends in the home lives of those who have answered the call.

*We need to teach our kids never to settle for something less than God's best, no matter how comfortable that choice has become.*

For instance, every parent is taught how to lead his or her child to faith in Christ, and we're always amazed how many moms and dads felt that they weren't "qualified" beforehand. This "Grace Breakthrough" course gives them four sessions' worth of practical tips and firsthand encouragement.

Likewise, Jeremy Hall, our student ministries pastor, periodically sends out an e-mail to parents giving them all the tools they need to engage in ongoing, meaningful conversations with their teens.

4. **Teach them that God's promises are strong enough to tear down walls.** Every truth that we have covered in this book can and should be taught to your children in age-appropriate ways. The power of promises discovered, chosen, and shared, the critical moment of a promise tested, and the concept of overcoming walls are ideas I have expressed time and again to my own daughters. I am constantly amazed at how they have been able to relate the concepts to their own lives, even at their young ages.

I have had the honor of sharing with participants at the first two national D6 Conferences—an incredible movement to help church leaders equip parents with the tools they need to win. (You can learn more at www.d6conference.com.) In fact, an entire section of www.FaithBreakthroughs.com has been devoted to help parents get across to their children the concepts of Faith Breakthroughs. More than just information, you can hear the stories firsthand of parents who have begun this journey with their children.

The best way to teach children to value God's Word, of course, is to value his Word yourself, to work hard at discovering, choosing, testing, and sharing his promises yourself. And when it comes to teaching about God's promises, you must take the lead. No riding a bike without a helmet and making your child wear theirs. No telling them they should search for God's promises without modeling the lifestyle for them yourself.

And the great thing is that as you pour love and grace into your children's lives and teach them about walls and promises, you'll be learning more and more yourself—and preparing and protecting them at the same time.

Since we've been talking about helping our children become wall breakers, I think it's only fitting that we end this chapter with an illustration from a children's classic, one that has a message for parents wanting their children to be prepared to make a Faith Breakthrough someday in their future.

## BESTOWING BLESSINGS

Do you remember the film version of *Sleeping Beauty*? The movie begins at the celebration of the birth of a new princess, Aurora, and three good fairies—Flora, Fauna, and Merryweather—come to dote over the child and give her their blessing. But before they do, one of them announces,

> *Each of us*
> *The child may bless*
> *With a single gift,*
> *No more, no less.*

One blesses the princess with the gift of beauty; one with the gift of song. But before the third fairy can give her blessing, the evil fairy Maleficent storms into the room and bestows her terrible gift: before the sun sets on the princess's sixteenth birthday, she will prick her finger on a spindle and die.

And of course you know that the last fairy gives one more blessing that eventually undoes the curse.

*Not in death but in sleep,*
*The fateful prophecy will keep,*
*And from this slumber you shall awake,*
*When true love's kiss the spell shall break.*

That scene ends with a chorus singing, "True love conquers all." And in fact, at the end of the fairy tale, love *does* conquer all.

While that's just a story, there's a very real truth at work—a truth that has the power to totally transform home life.

We have all fallen under Satan's curse, and all will die. But true love conquers all. For on Good Friday, when the Prince of Peace laid down his life, he made a way for us to live.

Teaching our children about love, grace, walls, and promises can awaken our homes to an entirely new level of joy and peace. And recognizing the Lord Jesus' place in the story is essential. He has the power to change your children's lives—and your own as well.

Investing time in teaching your children about the things that matter most is a costly endeavor. Going the extra mile to help teach your children about God's love will prove costly as well. But leaving a mark on your children that leads them to a love for the Savior? Well, that result is priceless.

## DISCUSSION QUESTIONS

1. How do you think the people around you now will remember you in twenty years? If you're discussing this with a group, share with one another how you believe you'll remember the

others in the room. What choices could you make to positively impact your legacy?

2. What are some ways to intentionally pass along God's promises to your children or to those kids whom God has put in your path?

3. If 50 percent of the homes in your community began to share these truths with their children and grandchildren at least once a week, what impact do you think it would have on those homes? On their neighborhoods? Churches? Our nation? What is stopping us from being part of that 50 percent?

# chapter fifteen

# LIVING FAITH BREAKTHROUGHS FOR A LIFETIME

I began this book with a picture of two walls. One was the Berlin Wall that went up in 1961 and stood for almost thirty years. The other was the wall that my wife and I have faced with our daughter Lily. As we close this book, I'd like to come back to both of those stories.

In the case of Berlin, the years passed after Barbed-Wire Sunday, and the idea that a heavily fortified, miles-long, heavily machine-gun guarded, nearly twelve-foot-high concrete barrier could fall in a *single day* would have been the stuff of fantasy.

But it did.

The wall was thirty years in the making, and hundreds of lives were lost trying to get over it to freedom. But the Berlin

Wall fell in a single hour. It did not fall flat, like the walls of Jericho. However, once word leaked that a breach had been made in the wall, it took only minutes for an amazing moment in history to begin.

Leading up to that historic moment, a bizarre chain of events had taken place. East German and high Soviet circles had begun theoretical discussions about opening the gates— an idea to slow the collapse of several Soviet Bloc states surrounding East Germany. Czechoslovakia had begun allowing East Germans the freedom to get to the West through that new doorway. Fearing a mass exodus, leaders had created new border regulations to take effect on November 17, 1989, regulations that were still very calculated and stringent.

Günter Schabowski, a spokesperson for the Soviet politburo (their High Command), had the task of announcing this plan; however, he had not been involved in the discussions about the new regulations and had not been fully updated! Shortly before a press conference on November 9, he was handed a note that said that East Berliners would be allowed to cross the border with proper permission. But he was given no further instructions on how to handle the information.

The regulations had been completed only a few hours earlier and were to take effect the following day, allowing time to inform the border guards of the new procedures. Remarkably, nobody had informed Schabowski. He read the note he had received out loud at the end of the news conference.

An Italian journalist, Riccardo Ehrman, the Berlin correspondent of ANSA news agency, asked when the regulations would come into effect. Schabowski's famously incorrect statement was, "As far as I know effective immediately, without delay."

Further questions from journalists brought up whether the crossings from East to West Berlin were to be opened, and Schabowski, again incorrectly, said yes.

Soon afterward a West German television channel, ARD, broadcast incomplete information from Schabowski's press conference. A moderator stated, "This ninth of November is a historic day. East Germany has announced that, starting immediately, its borders are open to everyone."

After hearing the broadcast, East Germans began rushing to the wall, demanding that border guards immediately open its gates. The surprised and overwhelmed guards made many hectic telephone calls to their superiors, but it became clear that no one among the East German authorities would dare to take personal responsibility for issuing orders to use lethal force, so there was no way for the vastly outnumbered soldiers to hold back the huge crowd of East German citizens.

Finally, one officer after another in charge of the Berlin gates simply opened them, stood back, and let a flood of men, women, and children pour into West Berlin. Without visas or passports, people began rushing through the gates. And word quickly began echoing among the West Germans that the wall was open!

There was a hole in the wall!

Soon every gate between East and West was besieged with an avalanche of rejoicing people from both sides, coming to celebrate the fall of the wall.

Some of the enthusiastic crowds started literally pulling down sections of that terrible barrier. Pictures from that night show that in many cases, the East German guards joined in with them!

The date was November 9, 1989, and today it's celebrated in a unified Germany much like our independence day.

Can you imagine? A wall standing for thirty years coming down in a single day! That's the power of a breakthrough. Walls cannot stand against words that offer freedom and life and movement, especially when those words are God's unchanging, life-changing promises that can wrench open closed gates and tear down any wall.

I hope that every time you see a picture of the Berlin Wall falling, it reminds you of the miracle that words—and in particular God's words—can bring to a city and most importantly to your life story.

Then there's the second story I tell in this book, the story about the walls Lana and I have faced in Lily's lifetime.

At the time I'm writing this chapter, we are incredibly grateful that the days of calling 911 in fear for her life seem to be behind us. The challenges are more subtle now. She still hasn't spoken her first words, and she's almost four years old. The trials of raising a special-needs child are unlike anything we've ever experienced. Yet in the midst of those realities, God continues to show us the way to victory over Walls of Fear and Doubt. That doesn't mean we don't constantly have to fight against new walls in moments when our faith grows strained. But the same God who tore down the deep spiritual walls of a paralytic in the Bible has proved time and again to us that he is the great Wall Breaker for our family, and our faith in his promises is stronger than ever.

You know now that both physical walls and spiritual walls can tumble and be cast down over time or overnight. But as we close, there are a few last thoughts I deeply desire to remain with you.

## WHY GOD URGES US TO REMEMBER

We humans are famous for short memories of both positive and negative events. Like photo paper that has begun to decay, the clarity and color of what has happened in the past can begin to be lost. Time and again, almighty God asks us to remember what's happened in the past. In fact, over a hundred times in the Bible he tells us to "Remember . . . remember . . . remember . . ." (Exodus 20:8; Deuteronomy 24:22; Ecclesiastes 12:1; Malachi 4:4; Luke 22:19; Acts 20:31; Ephesians 2:11).

In remembering, we experience again a part of the power of God's promises. We feel again his hand on our shoulder. His love surrounding us. His patience and compassion in dealing with our doubts and fears. And the amazing feelings of life and freedom when a wall goes down.

*The world is longing for pioneers, and your breakthrough could be the catalyst for a transformed generation!*

I challenge you to place physical reminders of your breakthrough in places where you'll not forget them: perhaps a framed declaration on the wall, or a piece of jewelry that you wear to symbolize the newfound change.

Most of all, I pray you'll share your breakthrough story with your spouse, with your children, and with others in your life who can remind you of your breakthrough on a regular basis. The world is longing for pioneers, and your breakthrough could be the catalyst for a transformed generation!

In the British army during the Peninsular War, there was a

group of soldiers who were called the "Forlorn Hope." Their name came from two Dutch words meaning "lost troops" because of the challenge they faced. Every man in the Forlorn Hope was a volunteer, and they were revered by the other British soldiers because they were the leaders who would run through the first breach in the wall of a besieged city.

These men were given a simple blue ribbon to wear. It was something a civilian might never notice, but every other soldier understood it was a badge of extraordinary courage. During the Civil War, General Sherman presented over a hundred Medals of Honor to a group much like the Forlorn Hope who bravely led at the Battle of Vicksburg. And the tradition continued much later with the World War II soldiers who were in the first wave to hit the beaches at Omaha and Iwo Jima. They faced enormous risks, but they opened the door for many more to follow.

*Never forget that what you do with God's promises will leave a legacy— for good or ill— for generations to come.*

These were the pioneers, the ones who could have stayed behind walls but who had the courage to press forward and break through into new territory. I don't have a wall breaker badge to give you, but if I did, you could wear it as an emblem of God's giving you the victory and of a wall coming down.

Being a wall breaker doesn't just impact *your* life. Never forget that what you do with God's promises will leave a legacy— for good or ill—for generations to come. Your attention to the walls in your life will have a profound impact on your children's lives as they grow up and face their own challenges. And I can guarantee you that if you'll just look around, God has placed friends and family and coworkers and fellow students in your life who will be inspired to face their own walls through your story.

In 2008, Malcolm Gladwell wrote a best-selling book titled *Outliers*, in which he identified the hidden components of culture-changing leaders. I am convinced that the spiritual climate of the world is transformed by "faith outliers"—people who have identified the invisible components that break down walls. Why couldn't you be one of those powerful leaders who change history? These are wall breakers just like you who never settle for less than God's best for themselves and those they lead.

## DON'T WASTE YOUR BREAKTHROUGH

I've told you of the power, security, and presence of a person who lives by faith and not by walls, but you can see it even more powerfully for yourself simply by looking at those people's lives. I hope you'll be a part of the growing number of wall breakers who tell their stories so that others they don't even know can be inspired. I can't urge you enough to go to the Faith Breakthroughs Web site (www.FaithBreak throughs.com) and write down your experiences for others to read. While I can't guarantee every one will be posted, I'll do my best to share ongoing examples of people who have used God's Word to break down their walls. Or if going online isn't something you do, then I urge you to capture what's gone on in your life story in a journal, or even set up a video camera and record what God has done in your life.

On the day the Berlin Wall fell, and for many days thereafter, one of the favorite things Berliners did was to take turns using sledgehammers to pound on the wall. In most cases, they might break off a small piece of the wall or just put a dent in it. But in their minds, they were adding their hammer blows to a wall that was coming down. It was a shared victory, and shared victories are always more meaningful.

## EXPECT BUT DON'T FEAR THE CHALLENGES AHEAD

It has been said that the definition of a fool is someone who is always surprised. It shouldn't be a surprise that if you've just had to use God's promises to knock down one wall, there may be a time in your life when you have to do it again. Either because the same wall that first came down has crept back up again or because of some new burdens you're facing, walls will be a challenge for all of you. If anything good comes from the Faith Breakthroughs model, it should be a refreshing perspective regarding the problems you will face in the future.

Every morning you can wake up with an opportunity to view life with the mind-set of a wall breaker. That is an incredible gift once you realize the impact it can have on your life story! It's not an attitude of pride or a "bring it on" kind of braggadocio, which sets itself up for a fall (pride doesn't bring breakthroughs, after all), but it's an amazing sense of calm and confidence that comes when you have discovered, chosen, and tested God's promises—and found them to be utterly true. It's beyond a "glass half full," Pollyanna view of life; it's the expectation that because of what almighty God can do in your life, the glass will one day overflow.

## BREAKTHROUGHS ARE CONTAGIOUS

I was finishing this chapter while on a plane with twenty-five other pastors and church leaders on our way back from Guatemala. These were men and women from more than ten different denominations from across multiple cultural and racial boundaries. And the trip all began with a question I had been wrestling with: "I know that people have walls. Do churches have walls as well?"

Of course, the answer is yes. And we're trying to overcome the walls that keep churches isolated from each other, and the people we are called to reach, by claiming God's promises that he desires us to live in unity, working together for his Kingdom. We often think of Jesus' promise in Matthew 18:20 as being for individuals, but in context, I believe it applies to his prayer in John 17:20-21 for his people to become one:

> I also tell you this: If two of you agree here on earth concerning anything you ask, my Father in heaven will do it for you. For where two or three gather together as my followers, I am there among them. (Matthew 18:19-20)

> I am praying not only for these disciples but also for all who will ever believe in me through their message. I pray that they will all be one, just as you and I are one—as you are in me, Father, and I am

in you. And may they be in us so that the world will believe you sent me. (John 17:20-21)

It is on the basis of that promise that several churches around the Austin area have made the choice to collectively adopt an impoverished village in the poorest region of Guatemala and share its transformation together in the days ahead through the work of the international relief ministry World Help. (You can learn more about this exciting endeavor at www.austinguatemala.com.)

Walls show up in every aspect of life, but the biblical answer is the same for each one: God's promises work everywhere they are applied. We're witnessing this principle firsthand in the areas of missions, education, the unique issues faced by active-duty military families, and more. I can't wait to see how God uses us to bring walls down in new and exciting areas of our world!

With those last thoughts, I'd like to close this book by praying for you and your family. If I could stand by you right now and put my hand on your shoulder, I would pray that the Lord would bless, keep, and guide you. That he would invade your family in amazing ways because of the courage you've had to face your wall. And I would pray that you will continue to be a wall breaker all your days, inspiring your family and many others around you, as you grab hold of God's promises and live a life of Faith Breakthroughs.

*Heavenly Father, I thank you that we have every reason to count on the promises you have made to us. Some of us are hurting, Lord, and there are people who feel like they can't go on. I ask you to give them today a new and fresh understanding of your faithfulness. Even when things seem to be falling apart around us, you have already won the battle. We pray from a position of victory!*

*And now, God, we resolve to live in that victory regardless of our circumstances. We choose to let you renew our minds so that our mind-sets will be transformed. We choose your promises over the lies that have held us back. We anticipate your blessings because you are eternally good. Even before we can see them or fully comprehend them, your promises will sustain us in the days ahead, for you are able to keep them all.*

*I pray in the matchless name of Jesus, amen.*

## DISCUSSION QUESTIONS

1. The Berlin Wall came down very suddenly after standing for a generation. Do you think the East Germans would have lived with a different mind-set if they had known how easily the wall could come down? In the same way, how does it change your mind-set when you understand that God has given you the power to tear down walls?

2. What are some of the most important promises you have discovered during this journey past your walls? What has made those promises so special to you now?

3. Are there people you love who are facing their own walls? What can you do in the days ahead to bring them the good news that their walls can come down?

# FAITH BREAKTHROUGH COMMITMENT

I began my journey toward a Faith Breakthrough on:

_____

## NAMING THE WALL

I am facing a Wall of _____, and
will no longer be satisfied being stuck behind this spiritual
and mental barrier.

*DATE OF DECISION:* _____

## A PROMISE DISCOVERED

I believe that God's promises can and will bring about
a Faith Breakthrough in my life.

The following promise will serve as a primary weapon
of faith as I tear down my wall:

_____

_____

_____

_____

*DATE OF DECISION:* _____

## A PROMISE CHOSEN

I choose to walk in the promises God has made me by making the following choices in the days ahead:

_____

_____

_____

*DATE OF DECISION:* _____

## A PROMISE SHARED

Even as I strike the very first blows to my wall, I realize how important it is to share this profound moment with those who will walk this journey with me. I will share this Faith Breakthrough in the following way:

_____

_____

_____

*DATE OF DECISION:* _____

## A PROMISE TESTED

Recognizing that in this life we cannot escape all adversity, I will prepare my heart for the challenges ahead, recognizing that God's promises have the power to turn my breakdowns into breakthroughs. From this day forward, I choose to live the life of a wall breaker.

*DATE OF DECISION:* _____

# NOTES

1. Information on the Berlin Wall comes from Patrick Major, *Behind the Berlin Wall: East Germany and Frontiers of Power*, (New York: Oxford University Press, 2010), 113, and Frederick Taylor, *The Berlin Wall: A World Divided, 1961–1989* (New York: HarperCollins, 2006), 94ff.

2. Ken Gire, *Moments with the Savior* (Grand Rapids: Zondervan, 1998), 116.

3. Frank Newport, "This Christmas, 78% of Americans Identify as Christian," *Gallup*, http://www.gallup.com/poll/124793/This-Christmas-78-Americans-Identify-Christian.aspx. Retrieved September 3, 2010.

4. Peter Robinson, *How Ronald Reagan Changed My Life* (New York: HarperCollins, 2003), 97, 105, 107.

5. "Remarks on East-West Relations at the Brandenburg Gate in West Berlin, June 12, 1987." Ronald Reagan Presidential Foundation, www.reaganfoundation.org. Retrieved September 1, 2010.

6. John McCain, *Faith of My Fathers* (New York: HarperCollins, 1999), 228ff.

7. Alok Jha, "Isaac Newton's Falling Apple Tale Drops into the Web," *The Guardian*, January 18, 2010.

8. Information on Alvin York comes from John Perry, *Sgt. York: His Life, Legend and Legacy: The Remarkable Untold Story of Sergeant Alvin C. York* (Nashville: Broadman and Holman, 1997). The State of Tennessee maintains a state park in York's honor, where Andrew York (Alvin's son) is one of the park rangers (http://www.tennessee.gov/environment/parks/SgtYork).

9. Nancy Churnin, "Actors Draw on the Life of a Real 'Shayna Maidel,'" *Los Angeles Times*, April 3, 1991.

10. C. S. Lewis, *The Lion, the Witch and the Wardrobe* (New York: HarperCollins, 1978 [1950]), 77.

11. Robert Fulghum, *All I Really Need to Know I Learned in Kindergarten*, fifteenth anniversary edition (New York: Ballantine, 2003), 120.

12. David Van Biema, "Mother Teresa's Crisis of Faith," *TIME*, August 23, 2007.

13. C. S. Lewis, *Mere Christianity* (New York: HarperCollins 1980 [1952]), 198–199.

14. Marian Wright Edelman, *The Measure of Our Success: A Letter to My Children and Yours* (New York: HarperPerennial, 1992), 7.